Making Group Work Easy

The Art of Successful Facilitation

Steven A. Schiola

ROWMAN & LITTLEFIELD EDUCATION
A division of
Rowman & Littlefield Publishers, Inc.
Lanham • New York • Toronto • Plymouth, UK

Published by Rowman & Littlefield Education
A division of Rowman & Littlefield Publishers, Inc.
A wholly owned subsidiary of The Rowman & Littlefield Publishing Group, Inc.
4501 Forbes Boulevard, Suite 200, Lanham, Maryland 20706
http://www.rowmaneducation.com
Estover Road, Plymouth PL6 7PY, United Kingdom

British Library Cataloguing in Publication Information Available

Library of Congress Cataloging-in-Publication Data

Schiola, Steven A., 1957–
  Making group work easy : the art of successful facilitation / Steven A. Schiola.
    p. cm.
  ISBN 978-1-60709-774-7 (cloth : alk. paper) — ISBN 978-1-60709-775-4
(pbk. : alk. paper) — ISBN 978-1-60709-776-1 (electronic)
  1. Group facilitation. 2. Cooperativeness. 3. Leadership. I. Title.
  HM751.S35 2011
  302.3'4—dc22

                                                                   2010032334

To my wonderful wife, Julie,
and my amazing daughters, Elizabeth and Emily—
thank you for your unending love and support.

CONTENTS

CONTENTS

ACKNOWLEDGMENTS

It is true that the writing of a book is not a solitary pursuit. Sure, I sat at the computer and put words to the page. However, to get from that very rough draft to the final published piece literally takes an army of people working toward the same goal.

It is also true that when thanking people for their help, one can leave out an important person and for that transgression I apologize in advance.

The work written about in this book is based on many years of learning, doing, adjusting, and learning even more. I could not have started down the road of effective facilitation without the teaching and mentoring of Bob Chadwick, Suzanne Bailey, Chloe Wolf, and Susan Sparks. I could not have completed this book without the expert advice and perspective provided by Dave Benson, Bob Slade, and Helen Ryley.

The book would not be possible without the countless and nameless schools, businesses, and organizations that trusted me to work with them and lead them through difficult times, possibility thinking, strategic planning, and conflict resolution. I thank them from the bottom of my heart for taking a chance on me and hope that the work I did with them left them in a better place than when we began.

I want to acknowledge the hard work of all the employees of Rowman & Littlefield Education for their professionalism and vision. Because of your work, this book is a reality.

Lastly, I want to acknowledge my dear wife, Julie, for slogging through all of the pages, helping me see the errors of my ways. Any grammatical or spelling errors you find in this volume are completely my fault!

INTRODUCTION

Yes, it is possible for groups as large as eighty people to work together to make decisions and solve complex problems. The key to a successful outcome is thoughtful, well-planned facilitation of the event. The purpose of this book is to provide the reader with practical, tested strategies and procedures to ensure a successful outcome of any facilitation event.

My experiences facilitating several diverse groups to their desired and successful outcome have taught me the wisdom and practicality of the steps outlined in this book. It is my deeply held belief that you too can learn to manage difficult situations and help others to solve complex problems. I have successfully employed the strategies outlined in this book with school faculties and staffs; groups of principals; employee groups negotiating salary, benefits, and working conditions; nonprofit service groups; community boards; a management team of a small city; and many others.

The latest research about improving education shows that when educators work together to examine data, brainstorm strategies, implement those strategies, and check the data again, student achievement rises. These processes are well known and effective. What is often overlooked or taken for granted is the process educators will use to work with one another and find effective solutions. It is easy to say that educators will just meet with each other and work these things out. However, as we have learned with students, people are not born with the skills to work in teams. These skills must be taught.

1

So if your work includes meeting with others to solve complex problems, you need two distinct sets of skills. The first set is the educational expertise and knowledge to examine data and develop effective strategies to help students learn. The second set of skills is effective facilitation that will provide you with a structure to have difficult conversations, ensure that all voices are heard, include all perspectives in the decision-making process, and make doable and measurable plans. While some educators think they have the skills to make all these things happen at once, the truth is many do not have the facilitation skills needed to work on the complex problems of student achievement.

As much as I would like to take credit for developing the terrific concepts and procedures found in the following pages, I must admit that I am a conduit with experience channeling these ideas to you. I've worked hard to cite the original thinkers who discovered, developed, and experimented with the procedures and strategies. A detailed reference guide is found near the end of the book so that you can learn more about the people and ideas that have influenced my work with facilitation.

Some people reading this book may decide that if they follow the steps I've outlined, a successful outcome is guaranteed. However, no such guarantee can be extended for the simple and indisputable fact that when using the procedures and strategies in this book, you will be working with people who almost by definition are unpredictable. However, I've discovered that when I diligently follow the steps that are outlined within these pages, more often than not the intended goals are met. Of course, that is the fun in doing this work! You never really know what will happen. So plan carefully, "listen" with all of your senses, and be ready to learn and adapt!

One last piece of advice before I begin: it is very important to know when to seek help with your facilitation. There are several scenarios that may require you to contact an outside facilitator. Here is a brief and incomplete list of some of the situations you may find yourself in that require outside help:

1. As a leader of a work group, faculty, or department, you feel your voice needs to be a part of the discussion. It is never a good idea to facilitate *and* inject your ideas or solutions. If you need to be heard, get someone else to facilitate.

2. You have facilitated a series of meetings during which no apparent progress has occurred and in fact you feel you are moving backward.

3. Despite all of the strategies you have used, members of the group refuse to participate and the process grinds to a halt.

4. You are involved with two or more groups who have galvanized into "camps" and are refusing to listen to one another.

5. The real problem is extreme conflict.

Having said that, I do believe that most of the situations you find that require a facilitator can reach a successful conclusion by the use of the strategies outlined next. Gook luck and successful facilitation!

CHAPTER ONE
THE ROLE OF THE FACILITATOR

The role of the facilitator is similar to other roles; however, there are special skills needed to successfully facilitate groups. These skills are often taken for granted. Excellent group facilitators make the act of helping a group move to a successful solution look easy. You may watch these experts in action and think to yourself, anyone can do that work. As with many other endeavors, one who is quite skilled at a task makes this task look easy to the casual observer. Just as a gold medal winner in an Olympic event makes his or her performance seem effortless, we all know if we attempt the same activity how difficult it is to complete successfully.

The purpose of this chapter is to make the essential skills that facilitators employ transparent to you. By doing so, you can take mental inventory of your skills and determine which skills you do well and which you may need to practice.

Many managers and leaders hold meetings every day. During the meetings, decisions are made, information is disseminated, and the work of the business progresses. Often these same managers think that if they are successful at running a department meeting, facilitation must be a snap. While some of the skills needed to run a successful business meeting and a successful facilitation event are congruent, successful facilitators need a distinct set of skills and expertise to lead groups. Listed below are the skills that a successful facilitator needs as she or he works with groups.

Deep Listening

One might say that every person needs to listen and we are built to do that act successfully. However, the kind of listening that facilitators do is not the same as recognizing your favorite song at the grocery store or restaurant among the other noises. The kind of listening facilitators need is deep listening.

Deep listening has several elements. First, the listener must be fully present. Often we listen only long enough to form the next thought we will say. To be fully present means to give your full attention to the speaker. Second, in deep listening the listener has the goal of completely understanding the other person's point. Third, deep listeners reflect back what they have heard to demonstrate to the speaker that they have truly understood. Fourth, the deep listener asks questions to clarify the point the speaker is trying to make in the service of complete understanding. Lastly, the deep listener is hearing points left unsaid but implied by the speaker.

Awareness of the Nonverbal Cues of the Group

Expert facilitators can observe the people in a group as they work and gather a great deal of information. They can determine if the instructions are clearly understood or the members of the groups are confused. They can tell when the group has completed the work and is ready for the next task. In order to "read" the cues of the group, the facilitator is using his or her eyes, ears, and intuition.

The more one works with groups, the more the cues they send are apparent. For example, one can tell how engaged a group is in a task by the sound in the room. When the members of the group are working well a low murmur is heard. As the group finishes the task, the noise level begins to build and the facilitator hears the change and knows it is time to move to the next activity. Paying attention to the nonverbal cues of the group is a big help to any person in charge of facilitating.

A great way to learn how to tune in to the cues of a group is to find a situation when an expert facilitator is working and ask him or her if you can work alongside. During the breaks and while the group is working, you can ask questions of the facilitator. This is the time to inquire about how the facilitator knew what the group was thinking or when to take a break. You can learn so much by watching from the point of view of the facilitator.

Willingness to Ask Clarifying Questions

Expert facilitators rarely rely only on their intuition, but rather they gather data to confirm a hunch by asking clarifying questions. If, for example, the facilitator is sensing that the group is uncomfortable about an issue that has emerged, he or she can ask these questions: *I am getting the sense that there is an issue in the room that many are uncomfortable talking about. Is my sense correct? What is the issue?* The answers will confirm the intuition of the facilitator and guide him or her toward the appropriate next steps.

You must learn to not make assumptions. Clarify any assumptions you are making by asking a simple question, *Am I to assume that . . . ?* It is when you make assumptions and act on them that you often find yourself with a problem. By clarifying your feelings and intuition you avoid acting on untested assumptions. When you confirm your assumptions, you also model the process for the members of the group so they can learn to test their assumptions as well.

Much of the work a good facilitator does is asking open and guiding questions. This technique is used to gather information and direct the group to the next activity. Examples of these kinds of questions are found throughout the following chapters in the book. Learning to ask good questions is an important tool in the facilitator's toolbox.

Flexibility

It is important for a facilitator to have a plan for working with a group prior to beginning the work. The plan needs to include the elements that the facilitator believes will help the group move toward a successful outcome. Most of the time the facilitator will implement the plan he or she designed fully and completely. However, there is always a chance that the plan will change based on new information uncovered during the work.

The facilitator is in an interesting position of knowing the plan will help the group and at the same time being willing to take a detour should that be necessary. The more experience one has, the easier it is to make the right move at the right time. Being flexible is a skill every facilitator must cultivate. Even if you take a detour from your plan, you will find your way back to the original path.

Knowledge and Belief That the Group Can Work Together to Achieve a Goal

It may seem silly to think that a facilitator must have a belief that a group of people can work together successfully. However, it is at the core of this work. If you believe the group can work together, then you will communicate that to the members of the group encouraging them to participate fully. You must also realize that people do not always know or use the skills that help them to work together. As part of the process, good facilitators build in short lessons to teach effective group work.

A Humble Attitude That the Successful Outcome Is Not about the Facilitator, But Rather the Group

Successful facilitators know that the work they do with groups is not about them, but rather about helping the group solve a problem or resolve a conflict. When you do this work it is a temptation to think that you, as the facilitator, must do all of the work. While you will be working quite hard, the task of solving the problem or resolving the conflict is up to the members of the group. You are there to implement the process, not do the work for them.

Your goal is to leave the process with the members of the group saying that they worked together to solve the problem. As you guide, teach, direct, and challenge them, the entire goal is to help them to work collaboratively and effectively. Resist the urge to do the work for them.

You may find this would be so much easier for you to just do it rather than have them struggle through the issues. It is in the struggle that they will learn the most about themselves, their organization, and their problem. Remember at the end of the process you walk away, but they must stay and work with each other.

Honest and Open Communication

You will find that as you facilitate groups there are times that you must be brutally honest. Such honesty must be accompanied by tact, thoughtfulness, and grace. For example, the group you're working with may need to face hard facts about their performance in order to improve. Or the group you are working with may not be willing to work effectively with one another and you must point that out to them and ask them to examine why this may be. Regardless of the situation, your role is not to befriend the members of the group, but to hold up a mirror for them so they can see themselves and the situation clearly.

You need to communicate honestly with the hiring authority. They have hired you to help the group with a presenting problem. It does no one any good to paint a hopeful picture of the situation. The hiring authority may be a part of the problem the group is experiencing and they will need to hear that from you.

Most people are very savvy about knowing when someone is being honest with them. They will surely see through any attempt at false honesty. On the other hand, they will trust and respect you when they know that you are being straight with them. As a side benefit, your modeling of honest and respectful communication will encourage members of the group to do the same. Only through the use of honest and open communication will the members of the group build a sustainable solution to their problem.

The seven skills listed in this chapter are essential to successful facilitation. The more you pay attention to and cultivate these skills, the more successful you will be as a facilitator. It goes without saying that these skills are useful in many other situations. However, taken together, they form the foundation of any successful facilitation.

You will likely see these skills embedded in the chapters of the book. Look for them when you are watching facilitators at work. Practice them in the meetings you attend. Learn more about the skills that are new to you. The more you facilitate the easier the use of these skills will become.

Concepts to Consider

- Specific skills are needed for a person to be an effective facilitator.

- These skills can be learned or enhanced.

- The more you facilitate, the stronger the skills become.

- There are seven essential skills that every facilitator needs. They are
    - Deep listening
    - Awareness of the nonverbal cues of the group
    - Willingness to ask clarifying questions
    - Flexibility
    - Knowledge and belief that the group can work together to achieve a goal
    - A humble attitude that the successful outcome is not about the facilitator, but rather the group
    - Honest and open communication

CHAPTER TWO
GETTING TO THE NUT! HOW TO CLEARLY UNDERSTAND THE PROBLEM

A journey of a thousand miles begins with a single step.

—Lao Tzu, Chinese philosopher

During the holiday season when I was a young boy, we had a family tradition of shelling mixed nuts while watching holiday specials on television. My dad had a bowl containing the nuts along with the tools to open them. He would ask us one by one which nut we preferred and then proceed to crack the shell to get to the meat of the nut. Sometimes the meat of the nut came out cleanly; other times he had to dig and dig to separate the meat from the shell.

It takes differing amounts of pressure and experience to crack the shell and reveal the tasty treat inside. Much like the nuts, problems and issues present among groups come in different shapes, sizes, and complexities. Many such problems take time and effort to bring into the light for the group to examine and address. However, no amount of facilitation and fancy strategies or protocols will help a group find successful solutions unless everyone clearly understands the purpose of the facilitation and the presenting problems.

Step one in this journey is to understand the problem. This is not to say that during the work with the group other problems won't surface that need attention. Rather, because time is precious, it is so important not to waste it following false leads or working on an issue only to find that the work you've done was for naught because a more fundamental problem critical to the success of the project was overlooked. While there are no foolproof ways of unearthing the real problem, there are three strategies that will help you, the facilitator, and the members of the group use your time wisely and develop a workable solution.

The first place to begin identifying the "real" problem is for the facilitator and the group to understand the context of the situation. This is easier for a facilitator who works in the same organization every day than for the outside facilitator. However, the starting place is the same.

Put aside assumptions and look at the situation. The facilitator, with the help of the group, needs to collect all of the information about the context of the situation. Finding answers to several questions, some of which are listed below, does this:

1. Is this a new problem or a long-term issue?

2. Who is involved in the problem and therefore should be a part of the solution?

3. What data do we have about the presenting problem?

4. If no data are available, what data do we need to collect to better understand the problem?

5. What are the working agreements of the group, mission and vision of the group, and the background information of the problem?

6. What solutions have been tried before? Did they work? How do you know whether they worked or not?

7. Has this group ever worked on complex problems before? If so, was that successful or not? If not, why not?

These questions are a short list of some of the things that need to be answered so that a clear context is seen.

It is essential that every member of the group understands the context clearly before you begin. A terrific tool for gathering information about the context is the "context finder." Using the template shown in figure 2.1, each member of the group fills out the boxes.

Context Finder

Mission Statement	Organizational Chart
Vision Statement	**Organizational Values and Beliefs**
Purpose of the Organization	**Organizational Goals**

Figure 2.1.

If the information is not readily known, members of the group are assigned to find the missing information and bring it back to share with the group. The facilitator can make his or her own Context Finder chart using the appropriate headings for each box depending on the problem.

A second strategy for understanding the problem is for the group to get as specific as possible about the problem. For example, let's say a group of teachers and staff at an elementary school is concerned about the reading achievement of students in the intermediate grades. Many people would present the problem as, "We need to improve reading achievement for the students in the intermediate grades." This is far too broad a subject and solutions generated at this level will lead to a scattered approach with limited success.

The group needs to get specific about the reading achievement of the identified students. Are these students struggling with comprehension, decoding skills, fluency, or vocabulary development? The members of the group need to dissect the data and find the specific issues affecting reading achievement. If the data to help them dig into the issue does not exist, they must figure out a way to collect the appropriate data.

It is important to emphasize that getting a clear and specific picture of the problem using data is not the job of the facilitator, but rather of the members of the group. In this case, the first few sessions will be devoted to finding as much data and information as possible about the situation and making sure that every group member understands the data and its implications. Only after a clear, detailed picture of the situation is uncovered will the group be able to make informed decisions about which strategies would help alleviate the problem. Remember data is neither good nor bad, it is just information!

A third strategy for understanding the context is the interview. This an essential approach for an outside facilitator. In this strategy, the facilitator will interview members of the group to determine the context and to look for patterns in the responses of the group members. If the group is small, the facilitator may choose to interview every member of the group. For larger groups, the facilitator will want to interview a representative sample striving to find as many diverse opinions as possible.

I am not advocating a long involved interview. Rather, I suggest that the facilitator ask three open-ended questions of each individual interviewed. Below are some samples of the open-ended questions:

1. What can you tell me about the problem or issue from your perspective?

2. What strategies have been tried to solve this problem?

3. What advice do you have for me as the facilitator of this group?

Take notes as people answer the questions. However, my mentor on this strategy, Bob Chadwick, advises that one should listen carefully and not take notes. His belief is that you will remember the important points and that taking notes keeps you from the deep listening that is required.

Once you've interviewed everyone, you review your notes or your recollections to determine the themes that were similar to all or most of the interviewees. In addition, you listen for and hope for the one or two people who say to you something like, "Well you know they say that this is the problem, but I think the real problem is . . . " If you get this response, you have struck gold. Often the real problem a group is having is not presented to you as the original problem. The "real" problem is the one that needs a solution for the intervention to be a success.

Remember that a fundamental job of a facilitator is holding up a mirror to the group so they can authentically deal with the core issues facing them. Sometimes during the course of a facilitation session it will become apparent to you that there is another deeper problem plaguing the group. This is often talked about as the elephant in the room or the cards held under the table.

Your job is to make the elephant visible and to bring the cards out from under the table. You may even have to interrupt the work to ask them to help you understand why there seems to be an issue no one is talking about in the room. Only by bringing these issues to the consciousness of the group can they move forward. More about how to do this is found later in the book.

It is essential that you direct the group to identify and understand the problem they are facing as they begin their work with you. It is possible that you may choose to use one or all of the strategies outlined in this chapter to identify the real problem. More time spent on clearly understanding the problem will allow the group to maximize their work and truly solve complex problems. The facilitator's job is to get everyone on the correct first step of the journey.

Concepts to Consider

1. Each member of the group needs to have a clear understanding of the problem before starting work to avoid wasted time.

2. Understanding the context of the situation is critical to the success of the group.

3. Get specific about the problem. Rather than the broader concern of low math scores, find out which specific areas of math the students struggled with most.

4. Conducting interviews with members of the group is essential for an outside facilitator to understand the group and the organization, and to get a sense of the problem.

CHAPTER THREE
ENSURING THE RIGHT PEOPLE
ARE IN THE ROOM

When a director is staging a musical play, she must find the people with the appropriate talent for singing, acting, and dancing. Only when the right actors are chosen for the appropriate parts is the production ready to begin rehearsals. But the actors are but one part of the success of the production. Stage hands, set designers, costumers, lighting and sound experts all play essential roles in ensuring a complete, successful, and enjoyable play.

Much like the director of the play, a facilitator of a group must ensure that the correct people are in the room. The importance of this task cannot be overstated. Many groups have done great work on complex problems spending several hours of their time only to find that a piece of vital information was overlooked or not even considered. This oversight has the potential to doom the project before it even gets started.

Let's suppose that a group of middle school teachers has identified a gap in the achievement data for students in seventh grade math. After identifying the gap and deciding that they must develop a plan to fix the problem, they gather together to address the issue. They work diligently examining the root causes of the issue and have narrowed the problem to a lack of practical application of problem-solving experiences for sixth and seventh grade students. While searching for a remedy for the problem, the teachers discover a supplementary curriculum that will provide authentic problem-solving experiences for students and decide to approach the principal about purchasing the program.

Two members of the group are selected to speak with the principal about the decision of the group, confident that she will agree with the group's recommendation. During the meeting with the principal, the representatives of the group find that the principal is duly impressed with their initiative and group work. Then the principal informs them that the district math curriculum department has noticed the same data and is working on the problem. Each school principal was informed of the plan in a meeting the day before.

Unfortunately, the district wants a remedy for the problem-solving issue for every school in the district. The math curriculum department is developing the process for determining a workable solution, so all math curriculum purchases to address problem solving are on hold until the district committee completes its work.

The teachers leave the meeting with the principal feeling dejected and angry, wondering why someone didn't tell them that there was another group working on the same problem. Later when they meet with the rest of the group, they all share their frustration about the situation and agree that they are much less likely to take the initiative to solve problems in the future.

No doubt sometime in your career, you have felt as the seventh grade teachers in the example. The sad part of the story is that disappointment and anger could have been avoided had the teachers thought more globally about the people they needed at the table to help solve the problem. Had they invited a member of the school administration or a member of the district math curriculum department into the discussion, they would have quickly learned of the districtwide problem and the broader attempt to solve it.

As you begin to assemble the team who will work to solve the problem, it makes good sense to stop and consider the people who need to be in the room. This is not as easy as it may first appear. The goal is to find the right people to bring diverse perspectives to the problem, but not have too many people at the meeting who feel they are in the wrong meeting. This takes thought and advance planning.

As the facilitator you must ensure that the people invited to solve the problem provide the group with most of the information they will need to find a successful solution. One way to find that diverse group is to ask, *Whom does the problem affect? Who is available to help us solve the problem? Or who will provide us with the information we need?*

As you answer these questions, you may find that the existing problem affects a far broader population than you first imagined. As an example, an elementary school is concerned about how students are behaving when they are not in the classroom. If you think broadly about the people who can provide valuable information to solve the problem, you will include paraprofessionals who supervise students on the playground and lunchroom; art, music, and physical education teachers who see all of the students in the school; special education and literacy teachers; and administrators. After all these folk are in the room, a full perspective of the situation is discovered and future solutions to the problem are examined from several perspectives leading to a sustainable fix.

Another idea you can use to develop a sense of global perspective is to use an organizational graphic to expand the thinking of the group. At one of the first meetings, explain to them that it is important to have diverse perspectives in the group to find a workable solution to the problem. On a white board or chart paper draw a large circle and write the problem inside the circle. Next draw lines moving out from the circle in all directions. Tell the group that you want them to think of all the people the problem in the middle affects. (See figure 3.1.)

As they name them off, you write one group or person on each line. When the ideas of the group are exhausted, ask the members of the group, *Are there people on any of these lines who have a direct impact on the problem who are not in the group?* The next question is, *Should we invite them to join us?* If the group agrees, then extend the invitation for them to join you. The combination of the questions that are asked and the visual representation helps to prompt the thinking of the group members.

The idea of including multiple perspectives in a group is not always easily accepted by some members of the group. Having an administrator in the group may cause some members to choose to speak less openly about issues. While this is a possible scenario, it is the responsibility of the facilitator to ensure that everyone in the group feels safe to say what is necessary to solve the problem.

Write the problem or issue you are facing in the box. Write the names of the people most affected by the problem or issue on the lines.

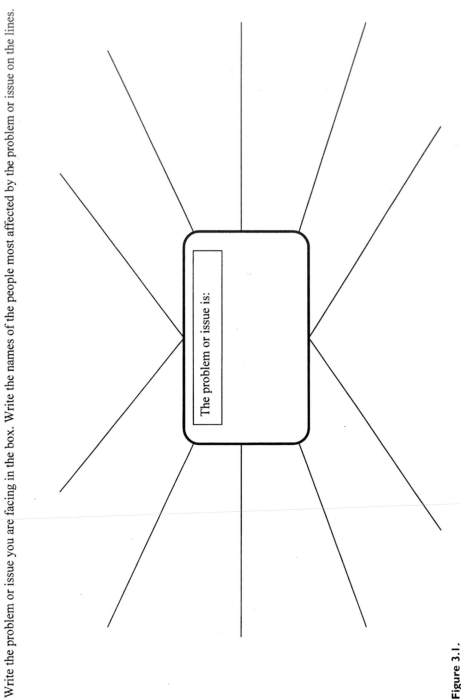

The problem or issue is:

Figure 3.1.

One way to do this is for the facilitator to speak openly about the need for diverse perspectives in the room and assure the members that every voice is important. Not everyone has a natural inclination to think broadly about issues so the facilitator needs to lead the group in this area by including diverse voices and explaining in clear language the goals that the group will meet by being more inclusive.

One word of caution: it is much easier to have the right people in the right places at the beginning of the process. It takes a great deal of energy and time to catch someone up on the work of the group if he or she doesn't start with the others. However, having diversity of group members and the best minds in the group overrides the work it takes to catch up a new member.

If you start working and find that you need other voices in the room, by all means invite them in and work to get them up to the speed of the others. In the long run, the effort of catching them up will pay off with a sustainable solution.

It isn't always necessary to ask people with specific information to be a full-time member of the group. You can invite folks with specific information into the group to provide their expertise, but they may not be needed for the entire process. For example, if you are on a districtwide committee working on adopting a new reading curriculum, at some point the committee will need information about how much money is available for the adoption. An expert from the finance department does not need to be present for the entire work of the committee, just long enough to provide the information and answer questions.

Concepts to Consider

1. Having the right people in the room to solve a problem will ensure a successful outcome.

2. Think in a broader sense about who should be in the group. The facilitator's job is to make sure that the membership of the group is as inclusive as necessary.

3. Consider who is affected by the problem and include them in the group.

4. Use the "perspective chart" to identify all of the stakeholders in a situation.

5. Group members can be added after the group begins its work. Make certain that the new members have all of the information they need to work effectively.

6. Invite people with specific information to present to the group. They need not be full-time members to help.

FINDING THE PURPOSE OF THE ORGANIZATION AND THE MEETING

The first step toward success in a facilitation event is to make sure that you and the group with which you are working understand the "real" problem. The second step is to ensure that the people who are most able to help you solve the identified problem are in the room together. Now it is time to make sure that everyone is clear about the purpose of the organization, the purpose of the group, and the specific purpose of the meeting. All of these elements of purpose need to be understood completely by every member of the group.

The Purpose of the Organization

An old joke in business schools is that people don't know what the mission of the business they work for is, but they know exactly where it is hung on the wall. Many workers go about their work without knowing the purpose of the organization for which they work. If you were to ask them why they do what they do, they will stumble around for an answer and basically land on the idea that they work to get money.

However, research is clear that in highly effective organizations every employee is keenly aware of the reason for the organization. You may wonder why this knowledge is important to a successful facilitation event. To get to the answer, we must understand that when we work in an organization, we are working in a larger context that has a direct effect on our work and behavior.

Understanding that, as a worker, I toil each day because I am preparing the next generation of people to be successful and contributing citizens puts everything in perspective. Now I know, as a classroom teacher, the assignment I give for students to memorize math facts is connected to a larger overall purpose of preparing competent citizens. This knowledge elevates the work the teacher does each day and ties the entire school and school system together as no single individual can accomplish this important task.

Back to the facilitation, holding this larger purpose up for everyone in the group focuses group members on the ultimate goal of the work. For example, we need to improve the reading scores of the third grade students in elementary school so that the students moving on from our school are ready for the demands of middle school and so on until they are ready to take on the role of successful and contributing citizens. In addition, for the entire scope of the work that is done at an elementary school each year, every adult in the school must work in coordinated action toward the same goal.

Therefore the role of the facilitator is to make sure that every member of the group understands the larger purpose of the organization. This task can be as easy as locating the mission statement each school has developed and making the group aware of it. Once located, it is a simple matter of making sure that everyone understands the mission statement and is willing to use it as the guide for the work.

Other times, the mission of the school is not clear or there is significant disagreement about the mission statement. Rather than getting hung up on specific words, send the members of the group on a search to find evidence of the mission or vision statement. Once the mission statement is uncovered and brought to the group, the facilitator's job is to lead a structured, but short discussion about the mission statement with the group leading to a consensus about the statement. Below are the steps for the structured discussion:

Step 1: Have the mission statement read aloud.
Step 2: Ask people if they have any clarifying questions about the mission statement. Have the questions asked and answered.

Step 3: Ask the group if everyone has a clear understanding of the mission statement. If so, ask if they are ready to use it as a guide for their work.

Step 4: If not everyone in the group has a clear understanding, ask those who have questions to state specifically what they don't understand and have members of the group address the questions.

Step 5: Once everyone is clear about the statement, go back to step 3 and move on.

Step 6: At the moment everyone is clear about the mission of the organization, it is time to make sure that everyone is clear about the purpose of the group.

Lastly, understanding the importance of the organization's mission statement helps the members of the organization and the group you are leading filter out requests and ideas that don't directly support the mission. Each identified problem or suggested solution will be viewed through the lens of the mission statement by asking and answering a simple question, *How does this activity help us to successfully accomplish our mission?*

If the answer is that the activity does not help to successfully accomplish the mission, it is discarded. If the answer is that the activity or solution helps to advance the mission, it is included as a part of a successful solution. Working with groups to solve complex problems can be a confusing endeavor. However, using the organization's mission as a filter provides purpose and keeps the group focused on the "big picture."

Purpose of the Group

Given that understanding the purpose of the organization is important, understanding the purpose of the group is essential. In our working lives we are often asked to become part of a group without a clear knowledge of the reason for the group. However, if you are going to put time and effort, especially if it is above and beyond your regular working hours, into a group, you should know the answers to the following questions:

- What is the purpose for the group?

- What will happen as a result of our work?

- What is my role in the group?

Many of us who join groups eventually figure out the answers to these questions during the course of our work with the group. However, we often attend several meetings of a working group and are still not clear on the answers to the questions above.

It is the role of the facilitator to understand the answers to the questions and communicate them clearly to every member of the group. In order to accomplish that goal, the facilitator must obtain clear instructions from the person or persons in authority. In preparation for the facilitation event the facilitator needs to have a conversation with the person in authority to determine the following information:

- What is the problem or issue we are facing?

- What is the authority of this group? Are we to make decisions about solutions? Are we to make recommendations about solutions to you?

- Do you need me to provide regular updates about our progress?

- Are you going to be a member of the group?

- How will you know that our work is successful?

- What will success look like to you?

As you gather the answers to these questions, you are then able to communicate the purpose of the group to the members. By being very clear to the members of the group about the reason they are gathered together and the expected outcomes, you can set the stage for the work and have a clear target for success.

In addition, knowing that the group is to make recommendations and that someone else will make the final decision about implementation is an important piece of information. That information will help you to know if you have to do the hard work of narrowing down three or four solutions to one, or if your work is done after three or four viable solutions are developed. It also will alleviate the possible conflicts that group members may have when one thinks that a decision has been made and begins to act on that decision while another member thinks that recommendations were made without the call to action.

Knowing the charge of the group before you begin your work is an essential piece of information for everyone in the group. As the facilitator, you may need to remind members of the group about the identified purpose when they get off track and begin working on an area that does not fall into the identified work of the group. At the end of your work, knowing your target will help all to see that you have accomplished your goal successfully.

The Purpose of Each Meeting

Along with understanding the purpose of the organization and the purpose of the group, it is essential for the members of the group to understand the purpose of each meeting. You may think that this is overkill. Just take a minute to think back to recent meetings you have attended, not led, and ask yourself this question, *What was the reason for the meeting?* If you can provide a ready answer to that question, then the purpose was clear. Many of the meetings we attend leave us saying to ourselves, what just happened in there?

Rather than leave the understanding of the purpose of the meeting to chance or interpretation, the role of the facilitator is to make that purpose very clear. When people know what is expected of them, they will work successfully toward that goal. In addition, it seems only right to be as clear as possible about the reasons for the meeting. This provides the members of the group with confidence that you are working in a transparent manner. Lastly, by being clear about the purpose of the meeting you are taking away doubt that can lead to conflict later.

Below are some sentences that could be used to communicate the purpose of the meeting. As you read them, you can see how by being clear about the task, confusion and conflict are minimized.

- At the meeting today our job is to brainstorm as many possible solutions to the identified problem as we can.

- During the meeting we'll decide on three recommendations, which we will forward to the administration.

- At this meeting our purpose is to clarify what data we need to inform our work as we move forward.

- This is the meeting during which every member of the group gets a chance to ask clarifying questions about the work we've done thus far.

- At the end of the meeting today we will have settled on a course of action that all of us will agree to implement over the next four weeks.

- As we are just beginning our work, we need to put aside our assumptions and look at the data with an open mind. Toward the end of the meeting, everyone will have the chance to share her or his interpretations of the data.

Of course this is not a comprehensive list of purpose statements. I hope you can see that by being clear about the purpose of the meeting, you are setting a clear goal for the group, giving information about what is expected, and eliminating areas where different interpretations of the work may lead to conflict.

Admittedly, not every meeting goes according to the plan you have envisioned. That is part of the process and to be expected at some point. If, for example, your purpose during the meeting was to examine the results of the data you've collected, but along the way some of the data collection techniques were legitimately called into question by a member of the group, you will most likely abandon the original plan and have a fruitful discussion about the validity of the data collected so that every member of the group has confidence in that data. In other words, you will need to monitor and adapt the process because you are working with people!

By fully understanding the purpose of the organization, the group, and each meeting, you and the group members will have a clearer understanding of the context, charge, and scope of your work. By doing this groundwork up front, it will allow you, the facilitator, to keep the group on path to find sustainable solutions for the presenting problems. While it may seem at first that this is a lot of busy work for no real result, the clearer you are with people about the scope of the work, the more successful you will be as a facilitator who can assure a positive outcome of the work.

Concepts to Consider

1. In order to do integrated and sustainable work, the group needs to clearly understand the purpose of the organization for which they work.

2. If a working organizational mission statement exists, use it to guide your work.

3. If a working organizational mission statement is not easily accessible, it is important to facilitate a discussion with the group about how their work will fit into the larger organization.

4. In order to facilitate successfully you need to obtain clear direction and guidelines from the administration or hiring authority and communicate these clearly to the group members.

5. Make sure that you are explicit about the purpose of each meeting.

CHAPTER FIVE
THE POWER OF USING WORKING AGREEMENTS

common nightmare for many is standing in front of a group of people you are supposed to lead, adults or children, looking out over the group to see that they are completely out of your control and will not listen to anything you have to say! Nothing you do or say will calm them and restore order and you stand there frustrated or run screaming from the room. Interestingly, there is a bit of truth in this nightmare. We have somewhere in our lives seen an unruly group and it scared us. We know we never want to get caught up in that situation again!

Humans are social beings. Even in the midst of the chaos of the situation outlined above, there is some sort of order. Someone in the group started to act inappropriately and others followed that lead.

If you don't believe me try this exercise. Remember a time when you joined an established group. As the new member of that group you most likely were on the lookout for the social cues that helped you to know how to fit in. You may have even tried a few things, such as speaking out in a meeting, to be told, "That is not how we do things here." It dawns on you that there are social rules to this new group and that to be a successful member of the group you need to learn these as soon as possible.

Most of the time the "rules" under which social groups operate are covert. You only discover these rules by close observation of behavior, or if a member of the group tells you about them, or if you inadvertently violate one of the rules. As a facilitator you will be stepping into a group with already established rules. At this point, you have a choice: should I just start the work and assume that everyone is aware of the rules and follows them, or should I choose to make the social rules explicit and understood by all?

To work successfully with a group and avoid needless confrontation and misunderstanding, the facilitator needs to make the social rules explicit and understood by all. There are three reasons for this choice.

First, as a facilitator it is your job to ensure that you create a safe working environment for the members of your group. In some cases you will be working on sensitive issues or with people who are in outright conflict with one another. By making these rules explicit, you can more easily ensure that safety.

Second, by establishing overt social rules, you will be eliminating some of the classic avenues for people to derail the process.

Lastly, people, as is their nature, will operate using social rules. It is better to accept this fact and work with it by establishing or emphasizing the social rules that you honor and believe in.

Many people call social rules *norms*. In the decade of the 1990s this was the most common term for social rules. However, it also became a joke for those who remember the television situation comedy *Cheers*. In that television series about the patrons of a Boston bar, a daily visitor to the bar was greeted by everyone shouting his name, "Norm," when he walked in.

Because of that interesting association, it was necessary to look for another word or phrase that described the social rules of a group. The phrase "working agreements" characterizes the concept of these behaviors and gives the facilitator a chance to talk about the agreements that the group will use when completing their work. This is the phrase I use in my facilitation work and how I will refer to this concept in this chapter and book.

As with the emphasis on stating the purpose of the meeting described in the previous chapter, you may feel that the identification of working agreements is a too formal or structured step. It is one of the most important elements in a successful facilitation.

The identification and use of working agreements demonstrates to the group that you are serious about conducting the work of the group in a safe matter. Working agreements are also the avenue by which you will address disruptive behavior and redirect people to the work of the group. Lastly, working agreements are the means that you will use during facilitation to encourage participation by every member. Working agreements are the facilitator's and group member's friend and ally.

Two Strategies for Developing Working Agreements

There are two basic philosophies about developing and using working agreements with groups. One philosophy advocates the development of working agreements from scratch with the members of the group. The advocates of this philosophy argue that only by developing the working agreements from scratch with the group will the members of the group see these agreements as their own and abide by them.

The other philosophy is that the facilitator brings the working agreements to the group and leads a discussion about them making certain they are clearly understood by the group. The facilitator invites members of the group to add other working agreements to the list. The advocates of this philosophy state that bringing the working agreements to the group saves time and the working agreements that are brought by the facilitator and those developed by the group will be very similar. Both philosophies have merit and will be discussed in more detail below.

The Process for Helping the Group to Develop Working Agreements

Helping the group to develop their own working agreements takes time. However, the facilitation process for this activity is straightforward. Use the steps outlined below to accomplish this task.

Step 1: The facilitator introduces the process by telling the members of the group that in order to ensure that they work in a safe environment the group needs to develop a set of working agreements.

Step 2: The facilitator may choose to give a few examples of working agreements to encourage the group.

Step 3: Members of the group are instructed to write the working agreements that they would need to work effectively and safely on a 3 by 5 card.

Step 4: If the group is small, have each member of the group share his or her list of working agreements as you record them on a white board or chart paper. Place a check mark next to those items that are already on the list but mentioned by another member of the group.

Step 5: If the group is large, divide the group randomly into smaller groups of five or six. Instruct each member of the group to read off his or her list while another member of the group records the responses marking a check next to similar items. The recorder in each group reads their group list as you record it on the white board or chart paper placing a check next to the item that is mentioned more than once.

Step 6: Once a list is generated from the entire group, ask the group to review the list and look for themes and similarities. Write the identified themes on another part of the white board or chart paper. If you have a list of five to nine items, ask the group if they need any clarification for the terms or phrases on the board. If they need clarification, ask members of the group to provide that clarification.

Step 7: Once the group is clear about the meaning of the word or phrases, ask the group if anyone would disagree with adopting the list as the working agreements for the group. After waiting for a minute and there is no disagreement, tell the group that these are the new working agreements for the group. If someone does disagree, make sure that you ask that person to provide a suggestion to resolve the disagreement. Once that process is completed, you have your working agreements.

Successfully Managing Disagreement

On an important side note, when you facilitate groups there is bound to be disagreement. This is not a cause for worry. However, sometimes members of a group may try to slow the progress of the group by disagreeing when you are close to making a decision. Rather than discourage disagreement, you need to let the group know that if they disagree with a point, it is their responsibility to speak up.

However, as a part of that disagreement they need to provide the group with an alternative. In other words, the disagreement must be constructive leading to a new understanding or idea, not disagreement that stops the process. This concept will become essential when you are making consensus decisions later in the process. It is good to model it early on with something like working agreements.

The Process for Presenting a List of Working Agreements to the Group

Step 1: Tell the group that it is your practice in an effort to ensure that you have a safe environment in which to work to use working agreements. You have brought a list of such agreements with you to the meeting and would like the group to adopt them.

Step 2: Here is a list of the working agreements commonly used when working with groups:

a. Honor Our Diversity
b. Work for the Common Good
c. Presume Good Intentions
d. Participate Fully
e. Take Care of Your Needs
f. Solve Problems Face to Face
g. Have Fun!

Step 3: Read through the list providing a brief explanation for each item. Clearly, some are easily understood. The working agreement Presume Good Intentions is defined as agreeing that if someone brings up an uncomfortable idea that he or she is doing it as an attempt to solve problems and not to antagonize or belittle someone in the group.

Step 4: Ask the group if there is further need to clarify the meaning of the working agreements. If not, ask the group whether they would like to add any other working agreements to the list.

Step 5: If there are suggested additions, first find out if clarification is needed to understand the word or phrase. If so, have the issue clarified. If not, then ask the group if there is any disagreement with adding the suggested working agreement to the list. (See the note above about disagreement.) Follow this process until the list is complete and there is agreement to adopt the list as the working agreements for the group.

As you can see, the process for adopting working agreements brought to the group may take less time than developing them from scratch. However, developing them from scratch can engender stronger ownership of the working agreements and can demonstrate to the group that they can make decisions as a group giving them confidence to continue with their work. Regardless of which technique you use, it is essential to the safety and smooth course of the group's work to implement and abide by working agreements.

Enforcing the Working Agreements

The working agreements are only as useful as your ability to enforce them. It is not a difficult process for the group to agree to working agreements. However, group members are going to be on the lookout, at least at first, to see if they will be enforced.

This means that it is essential for the facilitator to look for opportunities to enforce the working agreements. For example, if a member of the group interrupts another member of the group while he or she is talking, it is the perfect time for you as the facilitator to stop the person doing the interrupting and remind him or her and the group that we all agreed to treat one another with respect and interrupting is a violation of showing respect.

While no one likes to be reprimanded in front of others, it may be necessary to do so as the facilitator to model how the working agreements will help the group. After you made your point you may also want to remind the group that the enforcement of working agreements is not a job solely for you and they, too, are expected to remind their fellow group members about violations of the working agreements.

It may seem awkward or even demeaning to you when you first begin to enforce working agreements. At this point it is important to remember that you are working with people and that, while most of the time they will work in the group respectfully, there may be instances during the facilitation when members of the group have strong emotions about the subject under discussion. While feeling strong emotions is perfectly acceptable, it is essential that while sharing those strong emotions, one is respectful. If this is not the case, damage to the relationships among group members may occur, dooming the success of the project.

It is important to remember that some of the facilitation work you may do is with groups that are experiencing extreme conflict. In this case the members of the group need to feel safe enough to respectfully advocate for their point of view. It is your responsibility to lead the group, so do not shy away from acknowledging when members of the group are violating working agreements.

The establishment of working agreements is not an academic exercise to use when you facilitate groups. Rather, working agreements bring a measure of safety and equality to the group process. The establishment of working agreements allows the facilitator to manage the group successfully and the working agreements provide you with an avenue to address members of the group who are disrupting the group with their behavior in order to keep the process moving forward.

The use of working agreements also provides the opportunity for the members of the group to take responsibility for the safety and smooth flow of the work. There is not a better feeling while facilitating than when one member of the group says to another in a respectful way, "Remember the working agreements say we are to work respectfully, so please stop interrupting her." Very nice!

Concepts to Consider

1. Human beings in groups operate using social rules.

2. Because the social rules are a part of group interaction it makes sense to make those social rules overt calling them "working agreements."

3. Working agreements are used to ensure a safe environment in which the group can work.

4. Working agreements can be developed with the group or the group can endorse a set of working agreements brought to them by the facilitator.

5. To work effectively, compliance with the working agreements needs to be protected by the facilitator and members of the group.

CHAPTER SIX
EFFECTIVE DECISION-MAKING STRATEGIES

One makes a hundred or more decisions every day. Many of these decisions are made instantaneously without a great deal of contemplation. However, after a full day of making decisions, we are often paralyzed by the simplest decisions such as what to prepare for dinner. It is safe to say that most of us don't employ the same strategy for every decision. In addition, many of us would be hard pressed to describe the process we use to make decisions.

Unlike in our personal lives, decision making in a problem-solving or conflict-resolution group is best not left to chance. Successful facilitators recognize the need for the members of the group to completely understand and utilize particular decision-making strategies as part of their work.

Just as the structure for effective facilitation includes thoughtful understanding of the problem the group is to solve, the membership of the group, the connection of the group to a larger purpose, and working agreements, it must include a good deal of planning and thought about which decision-making strategies will be used during the facilitation.

This chapter will examine two decision-making strategies and provide positive and negative comments for the use of each strategy. Before we examine the strategies themselves, it is important to take time to understand the need for making an explicit choice of decision-making strategies.

Many times groups will work well at defining the problem, brainstorming solutions, and preparing to implement the solutions, but have not considered how they will make decisions. At the end of the process, for lack of a better plan, the group decides to vote on the best strategy to implement, leaving the majority of group feeling just fine while the minority of members who voted differently feeling disillusioned and frustrated.

Thinking of the decision-making strategies to use during the process ahead of time may lessen the feeling of frustration for some members of the group. That is why it is important to outline the main decision-making strategy you will use with the group early on in the process so that group members know what to expect when they reach a decision point.

Analyzing Data

The first step in making a decision regardless of the strategy you will employ is to collect, analyze, and understand the pertinent data. To develop a sustainable solution to the presenting problem, a thorough look at the collected data will guide the decisions and interventions employed at the end of the process. It doesn't much matter which decision-making strategy the group chooses to employ, the decision made is only as good as the information that is gathered and analyzed.

While the facilitator's job is to structure the process and keep the group members on track to a sustainable solution, it is the members of the group themselves who have the responsibility to collect and analyze the data. The facilitator's role is to make sure that the group members are examining a diversity of data and perspectives.

A simple procedure for gathering the data follows:

Step 1: The group has a clear, specific understanding of the problem.
Step 2: The facilitator asks the group to brainstorm a list of all the data they will need to examine to get a clear picture of the problem. The responses are written on a white board or chart paper.
Step 3: Once the list is complete, the facilitator asks the group to review the list and separate the items into two categories, "easily obtained" and "hard to obtain."

Step 4: All of the items in the "easily obtained" list are assigned to members of the group who will find the data and bring it to the group. The facilitator will ask for volunteers for each item.

Step 5: The "hard to obtain" items are reviewed by the group and a star is placed by the items that would provide valuable information. The group members make arrangements to find the data and present it to the group. Please note that some of the data is either too hard to obtain or not worth the effort and will be discarded.

Step 6: The group reviews the data and begins the process of examining it and drawing conclusions.

It is important to note at this point that the facilitator's job is to structure the process, coordinate the meetings, and keep the group members on track to developing a sustainable solution. It is the responsibility of the members of the group to do the actual work of finding information and interpreting it.

Sometimes, facilitators take too large a role in the group and must remind themselves that the group members must do the work to solve *their* problem. A simple strategy a facilitator can use when a member of the group says, "We don't have the information we need," is simply to say, "How are you going to get that information?" The idea is to remind the group that it is their job to collect and analyze the information.

Decision-Making Strategies

While there may be several variations, the two main decision-making strategies a group will use are voting and consensus. Voting is the most widely used and understood decision-making strategy. Consensus decision making is less widely used and is often misunderstood and misused.

Voting and consensus both have practical applications as well as positive and negative elements to them. The keys to successfully using either one are to make sure the group members are clear up front about which will be in use and to ensure that the group members understand how to use each effectively.

CHAPTER SIX

Voting

People have a clear understanding of how to make decisions using the voting process. If five elementary age students are trying to choose between two games during their recess period, they may decide to list each activity and count the number of children who raise their hand agreeing that they want to play that game. The game for which the most children raised their hand is the one they will play. This is simple majority.

Another example—the Supreme Court uses the concept of voting and simple majority to make decisions. If five members of the Supreme Court decide to rule one way and four members of the Supreme Court choose another way to rule, the Court will enact the ruling that the five justices selected as the ruling for the entire Court, next case, please!

Herein lies the largest negative element of making decisions by voting: someone wins and someone loses. As with the Supreme Court, the losing side, the minority, is granted the option of writing a dissenting opinion. However, that doesn't change the outcome of the vote.

This is not such a large impediment if the two choices that you are voting on are equally appealing. However, if one of the choices is quite repellant to members of the group, then the stakes are much higher. The group's members on the losing side are much less likely to accept the result gracefully. This fact is one of the reasons the Supreme Court hears similar cases over the years.

In some cases, groups will try to minimize the effect of the negative feelings by the people on the other side by deciding that the majority is not a simple majority; rather it takes a 75 percent or more vote for an issue to pass. The thinking with this compromise is that the group can live with the fact that only 25 percent of the people disagree rather than 49 percent as with a simple majority. The problem is that even though only 25 percent of the group is on the losing side, they are still on the losing side and may have strong feelings about that fact.

It must be mentioned that an advantage to using voting as a decision-making strategy is that the process generally doesn't take a long time to complete. Members of the group either raise their hands or vote by marking their choice on a piece of paper and the results are quickly known. You are done with that issue and now on to the next one!

As the facilitator, you will have some influence about how the group will make decisions. If you choose voting as your main process, you need to make sure that it is clear to every member what will constitute a majority. Secondly, it is your responsibility to ensure that all members of the group understand the choices before they cast their votes (see the process below). Lastly, you will need to think through the process you will employ when the minority does not accept defeat quietly and wants to continue the debate. While this may not ever happen, being prepared will help you deal with this issue quickly and respectfully should it arise.

The process for ensuring every member of the group knows what he or she is voting on is listed here:

Step 1: Clearly state the choices for the group.

Step 2: Allow time for the group members to ask clarifying questions about the choices. Ensure that the questions are adequately answered.

Step 3: Have the members of the group advocate for one choice or the other. Remind them that when they advocate they need to say something like, "I am in support of choice one for these reasons . . ." This is not a time for a debate.

Step 4: Conduct the vote either publicly or privately. Reveal the results.

Step 5: Restate the results by saying, "The majority of the group have voted for choice one. To be clear, choice one means that . . ."

Consensus Decision Making

Consensus decision making at its core is the process by which all members of the group agree to a particular choice or course of action. This is also the place where many people misunderstand the process. In consensus decision making the most common misunderstanding is that the group keeps talking until everyone agrees with the decision.

Rather, consensus decision making is a process by which the concerns and questions of the members of the group are answered leading to a decision everyone in the group can support. In fact there are three strong conditions that must be met for every member of the group to agree to a decision:

1. My voice was clearly heard in the discussion.

2. This decision, while it may not be my first choice, is one I can live with.

3. I agree to support the decision publicly.

When each member of the group meets these conditions, the decision is ratified and the group is ready to move ahead. It is important to note that the individual has the responsibility to be fully involved in the discussion prior to the final decision making, certain that the other members of the group understand his or her concerns and questions.

Another misunderstanding about consensus is that one person can refuse to go along with the group and thus stop the entire process in its tracks. However, the facilitator using the consensus process has the responsibility to ensure that this does not happen.

The simple way to do this is to help the members of the group know that they cannot just say they don't agree. Each member has the responsibility to speak up to make his or her opinions known.

If a person does disagree with the decision, the facilitator must follow the consensus decision-making procedure below:

Step 1: The facilitator acknowledges that a member of the group does not agree with the decision.

Step 2: The facilitator then asks the member with the disagreement to explain why he or she disagrees. Here is the most important part: the facilitator again acknowledges the disagreement and then says, "What do you suggest be done about the problem?" The dissenting member of the group *must* give a way to solve the disagreement. If he or she cannot, you move on.

Step 3: If the disagreeing member makes a legitimate point, the facilitator asks the group if anyone would disagree with altering the proposal using the suggested changes.

Step 4: If someone disagrees, go back to step 2 and follow the process again.

Step 5: If no one disagrees the facilitator makes the change to the proposal and asks the group if anyone disagrees with the proposal as it stands.

Step 6: If no one disagrees after a short pause, the decision is made and the group moves ahead.

Wording the question correctly makes a big difference in how people will react to the statement. Rather than asking, "Does everyone *agree* with the decision?" which may open the door for someone to just answer "No" and stop the process, a different way to phrase the question is employed. When the facilitator is ready to get a sense of the consensus of the group about the decision, he or she will ask, "Is there anyone who disagrees with this decision?" By focusing the questions on disagreement, it invites the group members to voice their disagreements and provide suggested solutions. A group member who answers, "Yes, I disagree with the decision," must then provide a solution rather than just saying no and stopping the process altogether.

The key to this process is that the facilitator makes it clearly understood that if you have had your chance to discuss the issue and you still disagree that you *must* provide the group with a way to move forward. If this concept is not clearly understood, then the results can be that one member of the group will stop the work in its tracks just because he or she does not agree. In fact, when a group is stuck, the facilitator will ask, "Is there a third way we can find to solve the problem?"

The negative aspect of using the consensus decision-making model is that it sometimes takes longer than simple voting to reach a decision. However, the positive side is that once the decision is reached using this method, the probability of members of the group successfully implementing the decision is quite high. When the three conditions of consensus are met the members of the group are agreeing to support the decision publicly. In consensus decision making, you do not have winners and losers. You are seeking a third way to solve a problem that may not have been thought of before.

It most likely has occurred to you after reading this last section that there is a third decision-making process one can use. You would be correct. Many groups choose to use a hybrid of the voting and consensus models in their work. In this process, you would decide beforehand which decisions you will make by voting and for which you will employ the consensus process. Typically, voting is used when the stakes for the decision are not particularly high. Often consensus is used to make the high-stakes decisions that affect the outcome of the work.

Regardless of the decision-making process you utilize, there are three keys to making decisions and having them sustain the group. First, it is essential that all members of the group have the opportunity to have their voice heard in the discussion leading to a decision point. Second, all members of the group must clearly understand the decision they are making and its implications. Lastly, all members of the group must agree that after the decision is made they will support the decision and move ahead. Only when these elements are present will decision making help the group to make positive steps forward.

Concepts to Consider

1. It is useful for the facilitator to present the group with a decision-making model at the beginning of the process and explain how it will be used.

2. A decision is only as good as the data used to make it. Data gathering and analysis is the task of the members of the group.

3. Participants of the group must clearly understand the decision they are making and its implications before the final decision.

4. Voting is often a way groups make decisions. Make certain that everyone understands what constitutes a majority. While it is a quick method for making decisions, there are always winners and losers.

5. Consensus is another decision-making strategy. In order for it to work effectively, it must be implemented fully. While it may take more time than voting, it allows every member of the group to support the decision publicly.

6. Sometimes groups use a hybrid of processes, voting and consensus. An understanding of when each process will be used is a key to success.

MAKING SURE THAT EVERY VOICE IS HEARD

As you have no doubt realized after reading the previous chapters, to ensure a successful result of a facilitation event, the facilitator must create the conditions of safety, openness, and structure. The elements of this process include

1. Clearly understanding the problem faced by the group.

2. Ensuring that the people who have the ability and knowledge to help solve the problem are in the room.

3. Connecting your work to the purpose of the organization. Making the purpose of the group clearly understood. Identifying the purpose of each meeting.

4. Using working agreements to create a safe environment for all participants.

5. Planning which decision-making strategies you will employ.

By thinking carefully about these elements, the facilitator will create the environment that will lead to a successful outcome to the work.

Now it is time to turn our attention to the work during the meetings. The goal of this work is to allow for each member of the group, no matter how large the group, to have his or her voice heard by the others in the group. It is at this point that the facilitator really begins to earn his or her money because he or she will work to equalize the time each person gets to talk and implement strategies that allow for solving difficult problems.

There are myriad protocols and procedures for helping groups solve their problems. The goal of this chapter it to outline the elements of successful facilitation that are used no matter which template or protocol is employed. It is important to have a checklist of elements any protocol should contain; this will help you choose the procedure that will best help the group achieve a successful result.

As with most things, one can find books with one hundred or more processes for facilitating groups. While these are a valuable resource, there are several elements that must be included to lead to success. Below you will find a list of the main elements followed by an explanation of the elements and its application. In addition, details of how these elements are used with large and small groups alike are provided.

Any process or protocol a facilitator uses should include the following strategies:

1. A process for hearing every voice at the beginning and end of the meeting.

2. A process for every person to have her or his voice heard during the meeting.

3. An organizational process for participants to work in small groups.

4. Public reporting of the results of discussions or brainstorming sessions.

5. A process that allows for contemplative time for participants before speaking aloud in a group.

6. The arrangement of the room for maximum interaction of participants.

7. Processes for recording participant responses.

8. A process for empowering the participants to facilitate small groups.

As we begin this section it is important that you know that the philosophy behind the strategies you will learn here is that participants of a problem-solving or conflict-resolution group expect the problem to be solved or the conflict resolved and they are serious about completing the work well. As a result, you will not find activities that are extraneous. Each of the activities and strategies has at its root the idea of moving the group forward toward a successful conclusion.

The process of ensuring that each voice is heard at the beginning and end of each meeting has three distinct elements. First, having an opening procedure at the beginning of the meeting allows the members of the group to speak about something that has low risk before they have to speak about high-risk subjects. Second, hearing every voice in the room at the beginning provides a period of transition for people. Often the participants of the meeting will be rushing from some other activity. The opening activity will allow the participants to put their previous event behind them and prepare for the work ahead. Lastly, the answers to the questions in the opening and closing can provide you, as the facilitator, with a great deal of information about how the participants are feeling and their expectations of the work. You may use this information to confirm your assumptions or adjust your activities. Listen carefully!

The procedure for conducting an opening and closing activity are similar. Follow the steps below for both the beginning and ending activities.

Step 1: After reviewing the purpose of the meeting, working agreements, and the agenda with the group, ask each participant to answer the following questions or statements:

- Please tell us your name and your connection to the organization. (This is only needed for the first few sessions until everyone gets to know each other or if you add new members.)
- What are your expectations of today's meeting?
- How do you feel about being at the meeting?

Step 2: Pick a person to start the process and indicate which direction around the group you would like them to move as they take turns answering the questions. Be sure to vary the person you start with and the direction you move around the group each time you do this activity.

Step 3: Make certain everyone has a chance to speak. Please note, it is the prerogative of any member of the group to pass. Should someone pass or leave out one of the questions just keep moving. You may choose to ask them if they have anything to say before closing the activity.

Step 4: Take notes as you listen for interesting or surprising information. Sometimes the answers to the questions can follow themes that are informative. While this activity does take time, the benefits far outweigh the concerns about time.

The procedure for the closing activity is very similar to the opening activity. It shares the same purpose of giving you and the other group members good information about how everyone in the group perceives the work. The key difference is that this activity is designed to be more reflective. The responses to the questions at this point are designed to encourage each participant to reflect on what was accomplished during the meeting. Follow steps 1–4 for the opening activity substituting the following questions:

- What did you learn today that will help you solve the problem we are working on?

- How do you feel about it?

When working with a smaller group (up to twelve participants), you can conduct the activities above with everyone in the group. With a group of twelve or more or if you are short of time, arrange the participants randomly into groups of five or six. Appoint one of the group members as a facilitator whose job it is to start the activity and keep it moving. Instruct the small groups to share their answers to the above questions.

When you think that most of the people in the smaller groups have taken their turn, ask this question, "Has everyone in the group had a chance to speak?" The members of the groups will let you know if everyone is ready or they may indicate how much more time they need. Make sure you allow enough time for everyone to speak before moving on.

It is essential that with every activity, you organize it so that everyone will have a chance to speak. It is important that you plan enough time for every response. You never want to be in a situation of cutting someone off or listening to two-thirds of a group rather than everyone. This will only breed resentment and frustration. The management of time is at play here. If you are running short of time it is better to end a bit early than to start an activity that you do not have time to adequately complete.

For small groups, it is relatively simple to ensure everyone has a chance to speak. Start the process with a member of the group, not the same one who started the opening activity, and move around the group inviting each person to talk until everyone has spoken.

Dividing Larger Groups into Smaller Groups

However, to provide an opportunity for everyone in a large group to speak you will need to divide the group into smaller groups of five or six. This is accomplished by randomly selecting people for the groups. For a group of thirty participants you can have people number off from one to six.

When the counting is done, the people who counted themselves as one gather into a group, people with the number two gather together and so on. You have just made six groups with five people in them. This technique can work with any number of people. You adjust the number and count off by the total number of people.

Listening with Respect

The second technique for hearing every voice in the room is insisting upon the idea that each person will speak in turn. Most groups will respond well to this process. To make certain that the participants understand the procedure, you must model it for them as you describe each part of the process. It could sound something like this: "Every time we work in a group, you will start with one person and let them speak. Then move on to the next person and let him or her speak. And then on to the next person and so on until everyone has spoken. It is essential that every person has a chance to speak. Please go in order and do not interrupt the speaker or debate them. This works just like the opening of the meeting."

After you have given the instructions, monitor the larger group or the small groups to make sure they are following your directions. Intervene only if you see that the participants are not following the procedure you described. Once in a while you will have a group that doesn't want to follow the procedure. In this rare case, you may need to sit with them and facilitate for a while.

Record Answers on Chart Paper

Another important element of ensuring that every voice is heard is to record each response on chart paper. This is not necessary during the opening or closing activities, but you will use the procedure for every other activity. If you are working with a group of twelve or less, you can serve as the recorder writing down each person's response.

For larger groups, you will need to make sure they are in groups of five or six. You will then appoint a recorder who will write the responses of each person in the group. When it is the recorder's turn to speak, he or she hands the marker to another member of the group and says his or her response, which is recorded.

When each person has had a chance to speak and his or her answers have been recorded, the recorder reads all of the responses aloud. In a session with several smaller groups, the recorders from each group each take turns reading their list until all responses are read aloud. In this way, every member of the group is honoring each statement by listening respectfully and hearing the information. It is essential that everyone listen respectfully without comment during this process.

As you can see, by taking turns during the opening and closing activities, and in the rest of the meeting, each person in the group has an equal chance of saying what is on his or her mind.

Strategies for Working with Groups of Twelve or More

As I mentioned in the introduction, it is possible for groups of twelve or more to work successfully to solve problems and resolve conflicts. It is true that it takes longer to get to the desired result with larger groups. However, there are times when having a larger number of people in the room is advantageous. Many of the same processes that are used with smaller groups will work with larger groups with some modifications. The main objective for the facilitator is to structure the work so that most of it is done in smaller groups.

When conducting the opening activity for the session, it is advisable for the first few meetings until everyone gets to know one another to ask the questions of the entire group. This is a process that will take more time than using smaller groups. However, the purpose of doing it in the large group is that the entire room will hear the responses, which creates shared meaning and purpose.

You can count on this activity taking at least one minute for each person so that a group of sixty people will take sixty minutes to complete the task. After the first two or three meetings, you can move to small group opening activities to save time. Because the closing activity is a reflective activity for the participants, it is easily done in small groups.

Strategies for Forming Smaller Groups

There are several ways to divide the larger group into smaller random groups. Numbering off, a process that is described earlier in the chapter, is one way. Other ways include, but aren't limited to, providing each member of the group with different colored strips of paper and then having the folks with the same color meet up; putting stickers, colored stars, or dots on the agenda and having people with the same sticker, star, or dot meet in a group; or placing colored dots on name tags, having people with the same colored dot join in a group.

It is certain that you can create other interesting ways to organize people into groups. The key is to ensure that you change up the groups for each meeting so that members of the large group have the opportunity to work with as many people as possible over the course of the project.

While the members of the larger group are now in smaller groups, you can conduct any activity that is necessary. The process is to have each person write his or her responses individually, share them with the small group while they are recorded on chart paper, and then the group's responses are shared with the entire group. The chart paper is collected at the end of the meeting so that the information can be transcribed and given out to everyone via e-mail or hard copy at the next meeting. The transcribed responses are then used to look for themes and issues around which there is consensus.

Developing a Draft Proposal or "Straw Dog"

As you can see, while it takes more time, the same work accomplished in a small group can be accomplished in a large group by using smaller groups as the vehicle for accommodating every member's voice. Another strategy that works equally well in small and large groups is to have a representative group work away from the meeting to design a draft proposal, often referred to as a "straw dog" or "straw man."

This draft proposal for solutions or policies helps to focus the larger group on the practical elements of the solution. It often doesn't take long for people to react to a draft and find agreement on some elements while rejecting others. The important part of utilizing this strategy is to ensure that everyone knows this is just a draft policy or solution and they will all have a chance to share their reactions to it.

Sharing Information Publicly

Whether you are working with a small or large group of people, it is essential that all of the work you are generating be shared publicly. You have already learned about the process for recording group members' responses on chart paper and having them read aloud for all to hear. In addition, having these responses transcribed and shared via electronic or hard copy is important, as well. The purpose of this process is to make sure that there is transparency in all of the work you are doing. These responses are then used for further work as you refine the solutions and look for consensus.

As the facilitator, your job is to ensure that everyone has access to all of the pertinent information so when you are ready to make decisions and develop actions, every member of the group has a clear understanding of the information leading them to support the final actions developed by the group. Remember the group members will need to be able to explain the process and how they reached the decisions that they are suggesting to anyone who asks them.

Individual Reflection before Sharing Responses

Not every person in your group is comfortable sharing their opinions without reflecting on them first. In addition, there are many times during the process that you will have the participants think of more than one response. To ensure thinking time and provide an opportunity for more than one response, it is advisable to pass out 3 by 5 cards to each person with the instructions to write his or her responses on the cards.

Make sure that you give plenty of time for members to write the responses. You can easily check with the members of the groups by saying, "Have you finished writing all of your responses?" They will let you know if they are finished or if they need more time. When it is time to share responses, the members of the group can choose to share everything written on the cards or just select items.

Do not collect the cards. People keep the cards, realizing that the opinions are theirs. They will only report out the items they feel comfortable sharing. Make sure that you have a handy supply of cards for the many activities you will do.

Options of Room Arrangement

The number of people in the group primarily determines the room arrangement and room size for facilitation. For groups of twelve or smaller, sitting around a conference table in a small room will work well. You must remember to have room for a chart stand with chart paper. For groups larger than twelve, you will want to find a room that can accommodate a large circle of chairs so that there is space for every member of the group to sit in one big circle.

You will need room for chart stands for each small group. When breaking up into smaller groups, you will need enough space for several smaller circles of participants gathered around a chart stand. If the small groups are placed too closely together, it is easy for participants to get distracted by other conversations. Tables are not a necessity for either large or small groups. They often get in the way. Group members will write on 3 by 5 cards, which is easily accomplished on one's lap. If you err, err on the side of a too large room rather than a too small one. (Please see room arrangement diagrams in figure 7.1.)

On this page are room arrangement diagrams that you can us as you plan the facilitation event. It is important to have all of the participants seated in a large circle for the opening and closing activities and for short teaching sessions by the facilitator.

Opening, Closing and Teaching sessions:

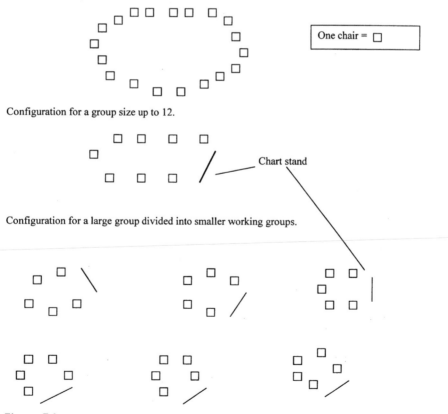

Configuration for a group size up to 12.

Configuration for a large group divided into smaller working groups.

Figure 7.1.

When recording the responses it is important for the recorder to write them the exact way that the group members say or read them out. This process takes some practice. It is important because through paraphrasing or abbreviations, important points and meaning can be lost.

Tips about Writing on Chart Paper

Writing things out on chart paper with a marker while someone reads them out is not an easy skill. With a bit of practice and encouragement, anyone can do it successfully. While giving instructions to recorders, make sure that they know it is important to write exactly what is said. You can joke that whoever holds the pen is in charge of spelling and can spell any word the best they can and it will be acceptable. Once in a while, a participant will be a stickler regarding spelling; teachers are notorious for this trait. Point out to them that the ideas, not the spelling, are most important. It is easy to sort out the spelling when the charts are transcribed.

Because there are differences in handwriting, it is wise to have the recorder read out what is written on the chart. After the charts are collected, they can be transcribed into a word document. If you or someone else transcribes the charts, make sure they are typed as they are written, only making spelling corrections when necessary. At this point it is a good idea to learn from the group whether they would prefer having the documents sent to them by e-mail before the next meeting or receiving a hard copy at the next meeting.

Procedure for Reporting Out Responses on the Chart Paper

When reporting out the responses on the chart, have the group members use the following procedure. Have them introduce themselves and read the responses they have written for the entire group. The rest of the group members are asked to sit respectfully and listen. This is not the time for debate or clarification. That process will come later.

Please make sure to stand so that you can read the charts yourself and ask the reporter to use a voice that is easily heard by everyone in the large group. You may ask the reporter to speak up if they are not

59

being heard clearly. When all of the responses are read out, tell the group what the next step is for the use of information and then move to the next activity. If the chart paper will be used later in the meeting, the pages can be removed from the tablet and attached to the wall using painter's tape that will not pull paint from the wall.

The facilitator must ensure that every person becomes a recorder at some time. A nice strategy for this process is that the recorder becomes the facilitator for the next activity, and picks the next recorder who has not yet served as a recorder.

Strategies for Providing Leadership Opportunities to Everyone in the Group

There are three main ways to get the participants in the group involved in leading sections of the meeting. The most obvious way is to have a member of each small group serve as facilitator for the group. To begin with you will choose the first facilitator for each small group. You then instruct the facilitators in front of the entire group about their job. It is a simple one to ensure that every person in the small group has a chance to talk. They may need to remind other members of the small group to wait their turn or not interrupt.

The second role the group members will take is recorder. That job was explained earlier in this chapter. Lastly, members of the group may play a role in working in a small group to design a draft proposal, or "straw dog," for the group to examine. Of course, every member of the group is responsible for participating fully and ensuring that the working agreements are followed.

Using Questions to Move the Group Forward

It is essential that as the facilitator you realize the members of the group are the people who are doing the work of solving the problem before them or resolving the conflict they are caught in. It is sometimes easy to get taken up in the idea that you want them to be successful to the point that you are making decisions for the group or designing solutions. While it is well within your job description to bring up difficult issues and to identify the times that consensus is reached, you must always check your assumptions with the group and get confirmation. Below are some sentence stems and questions that you can use to broach these difficult issues:

- I am getting the sense that there is another problem that we are not talking about in the room. A so-called elephant in the room. Is my perception true?

- My assumption at this point is that you are not ready to make a decision to move forward. Is this correct? If so, what do you need to move forward?

- I am not sure that the group can move forward until we talk about . . .

- Please check my understanding: I am seeing that we all seem to be agreeing about . . . Is this true?

- We are continually getting stuck when we talk about . . . Why do you think that is? What do we need to do to get unstuck?

- We have arrived at a decision point. Would you like to continue working this evening for another twenty minutes or would you rather stop here for this session and pick this up the next time we meet?

- Steve, you are saying that you cannot agree with the decision the group is about to make, is that correct? Okay, so what changes do you suggest so that we can move forward on this topic?

- I am not sure what just happened here. Can you help me understand? Just five minutes ago we decided to move forward with this idea and I see we are still debating the same idea.

- Hearing no disagreement with the statement I just made, we have decided to . . .

While this is not a comprehensive list of statements, you begin to get the idea that the facilitator's job is to reflect things back to the group and to make sure the items lurking under the table or left unsaid get said publicly. The words you use to do this help to continually put the responsibility of solving these issues on the group.

You may find that by working with a group, the desired outcome is not attainable. At this point, it is your responsibility to bring this issue to the group and ask them how they will solve it. As an illustration of this point, what follows is an actual facilitation event.

During a facilitation at which the issue was combining two district elementary programs into one school, the process was to find out the areas of agreement and disagreement so that the areas of disagreement could be examined and a solution developed. The end result was that the agreements and disagreements were outlined quite clearly. Unfortunately, the disagreements were too large for the group to overcome and the attempt to combine the schools was abandoned. The facilitation process made these issues clear and was used to try to bridge the divide. Sadly, it could not be done.

This is sometimes the result of the work you will do. Knowing that something will not work is good information for the decision makers who will then seek another way to achieve their goal.

In this chapter, many of the elements that are needed for a successful outcome of a facilitation event were explained. Several procedures were outlined that will allow all voices to be heard and for the participants to take charge of solving their problem or revolving a conflict. There are many facilitation protocols available to you after a short time for research. However, just following a protocol as you might a recipe will not necessarily lead to a successful outcome. The elements presented in this chapter are essential to any process or protocol you may employ.

Concepts to Consider

- There are many processes and protocols that a facilitator can use with a group. However, there are essential elements that must be present in any successful facilitation event.

- Any process or protocol a facilitator uses should include the following strategies:

- ○ A process for hearing every voice at the beginning and end of the meeting.

- ○ A process for every person to have her or his voice heard during the meeting.

- ○ An organizational process for participants to work in small groups.

- ○ Public reporting of the results of discussions or brainstorming sessions.

- ○ A process that allows for contemplative time for participants before speaking aloud in a group.

- ○ The effective arrangement of the room for maximum interaction of participants.

- ○ A process for recording participant responses.

- There are several leadership roles participants can hold: facilitator of a small group, recorder in a small group, serving as a member of a small group to develop a "straw dog," participating fully, and complying with the working agreements.

PUTTING IT ALL TOGETHER

N ow that the structural elements of a successful facilitation process have been outlined, from clearly understanding the problem to be solved to ensuring that every person has the opportunity to have his or her voice heard, it is time to put all of the elements together to design a successful outcome. In this chapter, a facilitation protocol entitled Current State/Preferred Future will be explained in detail to illustrate how all of the pieces that were discussed earlier work together to move the group to a successful outcome.

Included in the description is a sample agenda that would be used as a part of the process. It is important to note that while the process outlined in this chapter is useful for a number of issues, it not intended to be the single answer to all of the facilitation opportunities you will encounter.

Facilitation Protocol— Current State/Preferred Future

Suzanne Bailey of Bailey Associates from Napa, California, developed the idea for the facilitation protocol that is described below. I have adapted her original idea to make it fit on one page and have added my own version of the process (please see figure 8.1). This protocol has been used in over seventy-five successful events with groups presenting several different problems. It is especially useful in situations where

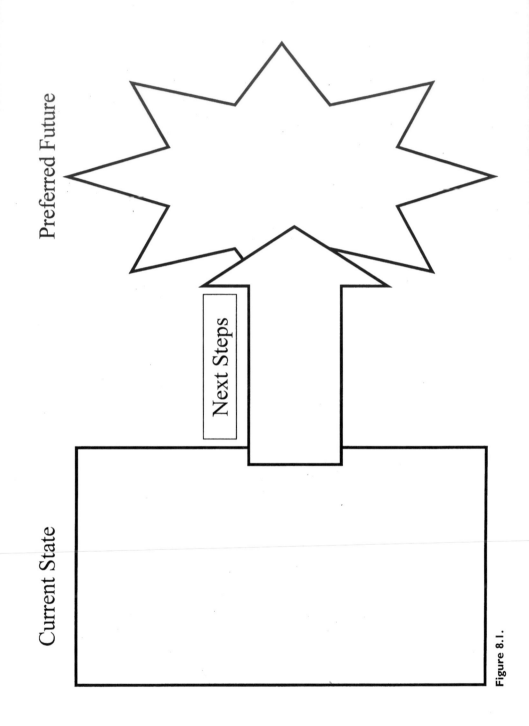

Current State

Next Steps

Preferred Future

Figure 8.1.

there is a vague sense of the real problem and/or when the members of the group have a difficult time finding solutions to the problems with which they are faced.

Before the process for using this template is explained, it is a good time to remind you that all of the elements discussed in the previous chapters are essential to include. Some of those elements will be easy to spot in the description while others are embedded in the process and while hidden are integral to the success of the event.

The Current State/Preferred Future protocol has three main elements that the facilitator will lead the group through during the entirety of the process. They are (1) defining the Current State of the group or situation, (2) discovering the Preferred Future for the group or organization, and (3) uncovering steps needed to get from the Current State to the Preferred Future.

The design of the template is quite purposeful. By having the three elements on one page moving from left to right, the participant can see the goal of moving from the Current State to the Preferred Future with the arrow in the center representing the Next Steps pointing to the Preferred Future. This visualization helps to reinforce the idea of the work moving from a place that is not working well to a new place in which things are working much better.

The first step in the protocol is to identify the problem. Second, you get the right people in the room. Third, identify the purposes for the organization, the group, and the meeting. Fourth, discuss and decide on a decision-making process. Fifth, develop or adopt working agreements. After these essential elements are in place, you begin work with the template.

Current State

The first step in using the protocol is to identify the Current State of the organization or group. At this point, you will present the template to the group. It is best to give a blank template to each member of the group. (The template in figure 8.1 should fit easily on an 8½ by 11 sheet of paper.) After everyone has received the template, you describe the process of identifying the Current State, Preferred

Future, and the development of steps to successfully move from the Current State to the Preferred Future.

At this point you will ask the members of the group to speak with two other members of the group and answer the following questions:

- Does the Current State/Preferred Future process make sense to you?

- What questions do you have about the process?

After allowing three or four minutes for the members of the group to talk about the questions, solicit *their* questions and answer them. Once the questions are answered sufficiently, it is time to begin the first part of the process.

The first part of the process, identifying the Current State, often holds the most emotion because members of the group are asked to describe the current working conditions of the group or organization. It is important that you do not lead the group to record positive or negative statements. Simply give the following set of instructions:

- "I would like you to use the template I passed out to record your answers."

- "Please write down your description of the Current State of the group or organization in the box as marked. Use the back if you need more room to write."

- "These are your responses. They will not be collected. You will be asked to share the comments you decide on with the group later."

- "This is a reminder that we are engaged in an individual activity, please no talking."

Monitor the group members as they work quietly answering any questions that may come up during the process. You will get a sense that most of the group has completed writing by observing their behavior. One sure sign is that people begin to look around, fidget a bit, or begin talking softly with a neighbor. At this point you will ask, "Has everyone completed writing your responses?" The members of the group will let you know if they are ready or if they need more time.

Now it is time to prepare to record the responses written on the template. The process is as follows.

- Tell the group members that you would like them to record their responses on chart paper for the entire group to see.

- Remind them that they are in charge of what and how much they share.

- For a small group, work your way around the table asking each person in turn to share one response from his or her list while you record the response on chart paper.

- For a larger group, arrange the participants into groups of five to six following the procedure described in chapter 7.

- Appoint a facilitator who will pick a recorder.

- Instruct the groups to share their responses to the Current State one at a time until all of the responses are recorded on the chart paper.

- Once the responses are recorded on the chart paper have them read aloud. For the small group, you will read them all. In the larger group, the recorder for each group will read out the responses.

The next step in this process is to have members of the group look over the responses and decide if they recognize any themes in the comments. In the small group, you can complete this process all together. In the larger group, ask each small group to decide on the themes that they see in the comments and write them on a fresh piece of chart paper. Only record the items that everyone in the group can agree on as themes. If there is an item that is not a theme, but a member of the group feels it is essential to add, have it added to the list with the consent of the entire group.

At this point, the themes are read out for all to hear. In the small group you would read them. With a larger group, you have each recorder read the themes for the entire group to hear. With the larger group, you can invite the group members to review what was read and identify similar comments made by more than one group. Members of the group can raise their hands and describe the commonalities they see among the themes identified by each group. Record these commonalities on another sheet of chart paper.

At the end of the process, ask if there is any disagreement that the list you have written contains the themes common to many groups. If there is no disagreement, you are done with this activity. If there is disagreement, ask the person or persons who disagree to suggest an alternative solution. Once that discussion is completed to the satisfaction of the group, this activity is completed.

If you are short on time, use this alternative process. Collect the charts and have them transcribed. The hard copy of the responses can either be distributed via e-mail or copied and distributed at the next session. During the next session, you will ask the members of the group to look for common themes found among the comments. Follow the procedure described in the paragraph above to complete the process.

The process to identify the Current State takes approximately two to two-and-a-half hours to complete. It is important to get through the initial process of having the participants write their comments and record them in one session. The work on identifying themes and getting to consensus on them can be a separate session. However, if you have to leave the process here for the next session you often leave participants feeling a bit negative. The reason for this is that while identifying the Current State, many negative or uncomfortable issues were identified.

When you leave the process at this point, participants are left with the sense that there are many issues troubling their group or organization. While this is not a reason to push the process ahead, it is an important occurrence to look for and recognize.

At the beginning of the next session, you may even choose to share your observations with the group and solicit their opinions on the phenomena. The good news is that when you complete the process for the

Preferred Future, these feelings move back into balance and do not lean so heavily toward negativity.

Preferred Future

To complete the Preferred Future section of the template, you will follow almost the same process that you used for the Current State. Participants will write their responses on the same template that they wrote their responses for the Current State. They will then share those responses using the process described above for small or large groups. Lastly, the participants will identify and come to consensus about the themes found among all of the responses leading to a consensus of the Preferred Future for the group or organization.

The one difference between the two processes is how they are each introduced. To introduce the Preferred Future, you will tell the group that they have successfully described the Current State of their group or organization. However, the future is not written yet! They have the ability to influence the future by what they do today.

The first step in the process is to identify the consensus view of the future. By following a similar process as was used to identify the Current State, they will describe a vision of the future for their organization. This is the time to think broadly about the elements of a successful future. The purpose of identifying the Preferred Future is to contrast that with the Current State and then develop manageable steps for the move from the Current State to the Preferred Future.

You may have noticed two elements during the development of the Current State. One is that the lists of responses for the Current State are quite long and the second is that coming to consensus about themes took time and effort. During the Preferred Future process the lists are shorter and it is easier to come to consensus. It is fun to watch as the group realizes that they have a very similar view of the future. It is a satisfying moment when they realize that they have much in common with one another. The issues that divide them become less important.

In addition, through successfully completing the Current State process, they have learned that they can work with one another to achieve a common goal. These insights will help the group develop reasonable next steps to move from the Current State to the Preferred Future.

Next Steps

The final phase of this project is to develop the next steps that will lead the group from the Current State to the Preferred Future. The arrow in the template signifies the section for Next Steps. Clearly, the space provided in the template is not large enough for the members of the group to record their responses. The good news is that in this section of the template you will lead the group using a different approach so the lack of space is not critical to a successful outcome.

This section of the template has many variations in the processes you might choose. Several options are discussed below. The main goal of this work is to focus the attention of the group on the shared future they developed by reminding them that they are in control of the future. By working to develop the next steps they will break from the current reality and move to the shared vision of the future. When the group bogs down or loses focus, remind them to review the elements of the shared future and continue to work toward making that vision a reality.

This is the point in the process during which the group shifts from identification of issues and the preferred future to brainstorming and problem solving. The first step in the process is to have the group look back at the themes they identified from the work on the Current State. Each of these themes may become the problems that need solutions to reach the shared future.

For example, the group may have identified that in the Current State there is a lack of consistent and honest communication. In the Preferred Future, the group identified a future in which everyone in the group communicates effectively and honestly. It is obvious that the issue of developing procedures and practices that encourage and support honest and open communication will help the group move toward their shared vision of the future.

To address this issue, the group needs to understand the reasons for difficult communication. So a hard look at the current communication strategies is needed. The next step is to identify processes and procedures that will ensure honest and open communication. This may take research into how successful organizations communicate or it could be obvious to the group what steps are needed to improve communication.

If you are working with a small group, you may want identify the issues from the current state and work on next steps together. For a large group it will likely be necessary for a small representative group to work on a draft proposal, or "straw dog," to present to the larger group.

Hopefully, during the consensus process about the themes in the current state, the group only identified two to four themes. If the group identified significantly more themes, it is necessary for them to narrow the list to just two to four. Otherwise the group is taking a big risk trying to work on so many things. They may find that none of them are done very well. It is at this point that your facilitation skills will be needed to help the group see that trying to solve ten identified issues and successfully implement them is a very difficult task.

Remember, you are only there to facilitate the group. Resist any urge to suggest problems to work on or solutions. That is the work of the members of the group to decide, as they have to live with the result of these decisions and make proposed solutions work. However, it is likely that the group members will feel energized and excited about making progress on their problems and may overreach. You will provide perspective and guidance only!

When the group is proposing solutions, you may need to invite people who can provide specific information for the group. For example, you may need to invite a member of the finance department because many of the solutions being presented have a cost attached to them. It would be demoralizing for the group to get their heart set on a solution only to find out that they can't afford the implementation of that solution. You may invite a manager or administrator to the group to provide information about whether the policy changes the group is suggesting can reasonably be implemented. Your goal is to make sure that the many perspectives needed to make and implement a manageable solution are considered early in the process to avoid disenchantment and frustration.

As was mentioned earlier, it is during the work on next steps that the group shifts from perceptions to reality. They are working on realistic and useful suggestions to move from the current reality closer to the imagined future. This is the place where the work of the group can take many forms. Below is a list of a few ways the group may go about developing next steps:

- The charge of the group may be to present to decision makers three recommendations for action. In this case, your job

73

is to help the group narrow the work to three of the most important recommendations.

- The group, after due consideration, may need to work on one of the identified issues at a time to ensure effective and sustainable implementation. In this case, it is your role to help the group focus on and develop one idea to implement.

- The group may decide that they can take on the work themselves from this point forward. They will thank you for your help and continue the work on their own. If this is the case, you may want to ask them if you could return in a few weeks to check on their progress.

- The group may turn over their findings to another group to implement. Your work is to make sure that they turn over clear statements of the issues they uncovered.

- Sadly, the group may decide after your work that the problems they face are too great to overcome. In this case, your work will be to help them separate amicably.

- It is also quite possible, through no fault of your own, the group does not successfully implement any of the identified strategies and continues on the same path they were on when you started. As disheartening as this may be, you must remember that your job was to help focus the group and structure the process. You have successfully completed that work. The real work of implementation is up to them!

As you can see, this part of the work can head in many directions. Some of these directions will include your continued work and other times your work is finished.

Here is an example of how the process works with a volunteer board of five people who identified a problem in their relationships. It seems that they were often bogged down in meetings with differing opinions and not much of substance was getting done. After going through this process, they decided that they needed to identify the ways they were to make decisions, adopt working agreements, develop job descriptions, and resolve a conflict present between two members.

By their next meeting, they agreed to clearly develop job descriptions and the two members in conflict agreed to meet and resolve their differences. They sent me a copy of the agenda for the next meeting, which included items for developing working agreements and a decision-making process, as well as clarifying job descriptions. My work with them was over, but I felt they were well on the way to making their preferred future a reality!

In the last section of this chapter is an example of an agenda for one of the meetings that make up the Current State/Preferred Future protocol. See if you can find the elements of successful facilitation discussed in this and earlier chapters.

Current State/Preferred Future Process
ACE Elementary School
January 29, 2010

Purposes:

- For the organization: To educate the whole child at high levels and prepare each child for success in middle school.

- For the group: Identify reasons for and strategies to improve the low achievement of students in math in grades 4 and 5.

- For the meeting: Identify the Current State of the math instruction in grades 4 and 5 at ACE Elementary School.

Working Agreements:

- Honor Our Diversity

- Work for the Common Good

- Presume Good Intentions

- Participate Fully

- Take Care of Your Needs

- Solve Problems Face to Face

- Have Fun!

Agenda:

- Review of Purposes, Working Agreements, and Agenda.

- Opening Activity: Please answer the following questions:
  - Introduce yourself and your relationship to the school.
  - What are your expectations of this meeting?
  - How do you feel about being here?

- Description of and consensus about the decision-making model used by the group.

- Description of the Current State/Preferred Future process and distribution of the template.

- Participants write their description of the Current State on the template.

- Report out the descriptions of the Current State.

- Discussion of themes found in comments.

- Closing Activity: Please share your answers to the following questions:
  - What did you learn today that would help you solve the problem of low math achievement?
  - How do you feel about it?

Next meeting: February 15 at 3 p.m.

Were you able to find several elements that have been described in the book thus far?

This type of agenda has proven to be quite successful for many different meetings. You can use it as a template on your computer, changing the pertinent information for the meeting you are conducting as necessary!

Concepts to Consider

- A complex facilitation protocol includes all of the elements of successful facilitation discussed in previous chapters.

- The process of identifying the Current State involves individual, small group, and whole group work.

- The process of identifying the Preferred Future involves individual, small group, and whole group work.

- The development of Next Steps to move from the Current State to the Preferred Future can take many forms; some of them may not involve you.

- The Current State/Preferred Future protocol is just one of many facilitation protocols you may choose to use.

- The agenda for a meeting contains the following elements: purposes of the organization, group, and meeting; working agreements; and a detailed agenda.

EVALUATION AND ACCOUNTABILITY

The hard work of guiding a group to a successful outcome, especially when they were facing a difficult problem or conflict to resolve, is possible by creating a safe structure in which the members of the group can work and using the facilitation skills you've read about in previous chapters. It is a wonderful feeling a facilitator experiences when she or he has successfully shepherded the group. However, and you knew this was coming, this is where the real work for the group members begins. It is one thing to discuss issues and decide on interventions and strategies in the group. It is quite another to implement the agreed-upon strategies successfully in the larger organization.

It is important to remind yourself that, as the facilitator, it is not your job to implement the strategies. You can have some influence with the group before you end your work with them. Helping the members of the group to thoughtfully build in evaluation and accountability components to their work is essential to successful implementation of the strategies they have designed.

The work the facilitator does at this point is explaining clearly to the group the reasons for working a bit longer together to include accountability and evaluation components. There are many different activities that you can lead the group through to help them develop the evaluation and accountability measures that will increase the possibility of successful implementation.

Many times the members of the group have worked hard finding consensus about the important issues facing them. They often are tired and don't want to put more energy into the process. However, just as groups of people need guidance to work successfully, they also need to have clear targets to hit, places along the way to objectively check their progress, and a clear understanding of who is responsible for which tasks. The truth of the matter is that the process is not fully completed until this work is done.

There are two basic areas in which to begin the work of evaluation and accountability. One area is to answer the following question, *Who will do what by when?* The other area of evaluation is to help the group clearly determine what success would look and feel like when the strategies they developed are fully implemented.

By having a clear picture of success, the members of the implementation team will look to milestones and markers to check their progress toward their preferred vision. The rest of this chapter will focus on the activities that will successfully lead you and the group as you complete these important tasks.

Before we get to the description of the activities, it is important to pause for a minute to consider a real example of how this process will work with a group. A volunteer board of a community organization wanted to develop a more unified and focused vision for their work. They were clear that they did not want to micromanage the leadership team, but they did have grand plans to expand their reach into other communities and to update and remodel current facilities.

The past history of the board was that they were selected for their ability to bring donations to the cause. While this is important to any nonprofit community organization, the board wanted a more unified front and deeper involvement in the organization. The leadership team was excited about the energy and enthusiasm the board members were bringing to the task. However, they were a bit skeptical and concerned about the many diverse ideas that were developed during a brainstorming session at the previous board meeting.

The management team and the board members agreed to attend a facilitated full-day retreat at which they would develop the beginnings of a strategic plan and vision for the future. During the planning for the retreat, it was decided that the Current State/Preferred Future process would guide the work at the retreat.

The purpose of the meeting was clearly described for all of the attendees. The board members, the leadership team, and the staff of the organization were invited to attend. After a description of the purpose and the process used in the meeting, the members of the assembled group participated in the opening activity. Shortly after that, the process of developing a Current State was begun. It became clear that there were several important issues that needed attention, including the state of the facilities currently in use.

The next step was to determine the Preferred Future of the organization. After participating in the process, the group realized that they held many of the same ideas about the future of the organization. It was then time to develop the steps that would lead the group from where they were to where they wanted to be in the future. Many next steps were developed and agreed upon. The last step before the group adjourned for the day was to decide on what success would look like and who would do what by when. The board members and staff volunteered to take on specific tasks that were designed to lead them to the desired outcome.

At each subsequent board meeting an agenda item was added during which the progress toward the identified goals was discussed. As a result of the work of the board and staff, a new building was built in an adjacent town and plans for remodeling another center were developed.

As you can see, the best of intentions are not enough to effect positive change. The intentions need to be coupled with concrete steps designed to move the group toward their identified vision. The other important outcome of the work the above group did on next steps was that they discovered that every member of the board and staff had an important role to play in making the Preferred Future a reality. This realization of a role for everyone leads to a sense of empowerment and positive contribution felt within the group.

So the question is, how do you facilitate the group so that they happily develop accountability and evaluation of their work? Developing accountability is a simple process of first identifying the main tasks that need to be done and matching those tasks to members of the group who will complete them.

The first question to ask in this process is *what do you need to do to begin work on the next steps?* The process for identifying these steps is quite simple. First you have the group members identify and come to consensus on the important tasks needed to make progress toward the Preferred Future. Then the facilitator leads the group through a process of prioritizing the tasks focusing on those that are key to successful implementation of the identified next steps.

Once the group has reached consensus on the identified tasks, the next step is to match names and dates to each of the identified tasks. Remember you are working to answer the question, *who does what by when?* A simple process for keeping track of the tasks, times, and people who will complete them is to use a chart like the one in figure 9.1. Use this chart once the Next Steps of the Current State/Preferred Future process is completed. Write the names of the persons who will be responsible to complete the task, a short description of the task, and the estimated date of completion in the chart. Place a check mark and the date completed in the last column.

Once the chart is completed, a copy is distributed to every member in the group and to the administration. It then becomes the responsibility of the members of the group to monitor the progress made toward accomplishing the stated next steps. Typically, the group will meet periodically to discuss the progress toward the next steps.

It is important to note that the interventions or strategies developed during the problem-solving or conflict-resolution process are the group's best guess about what will work to solve their problem. At the time the interventions were developed, it was impossible to predict whether they would effectively solve the problem. The role of the facilitator is to make a statement to the group that a good reason for monitoring the progress of the interventions is to make adjustments or corrections to the interventions.

While the interventions represent the best thinking of the group, only by trying the suggestions and looking for evidence that the process is working will they know if the intervention is successful. They may see an intervention that is not working and become discouraged. Remind them that just because one intervention is not working the way they had hoped it is not time to give up on the process. Rather, it is time to adjust their strategies or try a new strategy altogether.

The next step in establishing an accountability system is to define the success for the work. If you use the Current State/Preferred Future

Accountability—Documenting Who Does What by When

Task number	Name of Person Completing Task	Short Description of the Task	When the Task Will Be Completed	Date of Actual Completion of Task
1				
2				
3				
4				
5				
6				
7				
8				
9				
10				

Figure 9.1.

process, the group will have developed a consensus view of the future. They may tell you that success is achieving the Preferred Future. That is true as far as it goes. You need to help them realize that the Preferred Future is not easy to obtain and in order to know that they are making progress toward their goal, they need to have signposts along the way.

The procedure for defining success is to examine each of the identified next steps and to ask the question, *how will we know if we've achieved this goal successfully?* At this point the members of the group will provide ways to measure progress. For some of the items on the list this process will be quite easy. For example, if it was determined that a next step for the group is to adopt a set of working agreements to be used every time they meet, then the establishment of working agreements will meet this goal. However, if one of the identified next steps of the group was to change instructional strategies for reading to find a greater impact on student achievement, then the evaluation of that goal will have many more steps.

For the goal about improving reading achievement of students, the group may suggest having each student take an Independent Reading Inventory before the intervention begins. After three weeks, the same students are tested again and the group examines the data generated by the tests. If significant progress is found, they may decide to keep the intervention in place. However, if significant progress is not found, they may choose to implement a different intervention. The same question will be asked, *how will you know that you reached your goal?*

This may seem like a tedious process. However, you will need to remind the group that they invested a great deal of time working with one another to address the presenting problem. Without follow-up and evaluation, how will they know that the work they did was useful?

In your role as the facilitator, the best you can hope for is that you've planted the seeds and modeled the use of evaluation and accountability. It is now the responsibility of the group to implement the agreed-upon plans.

To review, for each of the identified next steps, the group will decide on benchmarks that will demonstrate progress toward the goal. The group needs to be aware that if the benchmarks do not show progress, they will need to adjust their plans accordingly. An example of this procedure is detailed below.

Next Steps:

- The group will adopt and use working agreements every time they meet.
  - Success: We will adopt working agreements at the next meeting. We will use them at every meeting.
- The group will agree on a decision-making process and use it at each meeting.
  - Success: We have decided on a consensus decision-making model at the next meeting. We use it to make the main decision in the group.
- The group will define responsibilities for each job.
  - Success: Each job has a written job description in place within thirty days.
- We will implement direct instruction of comprehension skills for all fourth and fifth grade students who are not on grade level in reading.
  - Success: We will give the identified students a comprehension test prior to the start of instruction.
  - After three weeks, the students will take the same comprehension test and the scores will be examined to determine student achievement growth. (See figure 9.2 to view a template for this activity.)

Of course these are but some of the many next steps the group may develop. The key point is that for each next step there needs to be a corresponding indicator of success. Sometimes group members are reluctant to set firm goals because they are worried about what might happen if they do not meet their goals. This is a real concern for people who've never worked with this type of accountability process.

While it is impossible to alleviate fear altogether, your job is to assure them that the ultimate goal is to get to the Preferred Future. So, if one intervention doesn't work, that tells them some information and allows them to try another intervention. The idea is to keep working

Defining Success

An important aspect of accountability is the definition of success. On this page are some examples of tools you can use to help groups define the success of the interventions they developed during the Next Steps of the facilitation procedure.

A success statement with timeline, percentage improvement, and measurement tool:

By _____ (date), the _____ (subject of the intervention) will improve by _____ (a percentage) as measured by _____ (assessment procedure or test).

Please note that it is important to include a reasonable and doable number in the percentage of improvement because it provides a target for the group to hit and indicates a measure of success.

A list of activities that indicate success:

Use this list of activities to indicate how the group will know they achieved success with the identified interventions.

Success looks like

    1.
    2.
    3.

A success statement:

The group will write a statement that will indicate the conditions for success. It may start like this: We know that the intervention has achieved success when we can see . . .

Figure 9.2.

toward the identified goals. This fear won't be quieted until they have experienced the process fully.

There are many processes that can be utilized to build in the elements of evaluation and accountability. The processes mentioned in this chapter are but just two. The important point is that the work is not done until an accountability process is built in.

When you are first speaking with the decision makers about taking the job of facilitating the group, one of the main questions you need to ask is, *what will success look like for you?* When the group is contemplating the next steps, it is a good time to review your initial notes on the job to see that the success markers the decision makers wanted to see are present in the final product. Most times the decision makers want the conflict resolved or a decision made. Therefore, if you work the plan, you will accomplish those goals.

Concepts to Consider

- The work of the group is not finished until each identified next step has a statement or two about what success with that step will look like.

- To ensure accountability, the group will need to answer the question, *who will do what by when?*

- A chart with the answers to these questions is a nice tool to keep track of the work.

- Using a process during which the group looks at each next step and develops a statement that indicates what success will look like is important to ensuring accountability and showing progress.

- The group needs to understand that the development of the next steps is their best guess. If they implement one of their ideas and it does not work the way they had hoped, they need to continue to look for other strategies that may help.

CHAPTER TEN
LOOKING FOR AND CELEBRATING SUCCESS

B y now you have finished the facilitation process and the members of the group are happily back to work. You have assured that accountability and evaluation have been built into the work. The members of the group, in addition to their other jobs, are working on the next steps that were developed during the facilitation process. The decision makers who hired you to facilitate the group are excited about the resolution of the main problem and are impressed with the positive attitude of the members about their time in the group. So you say to yourself with a satisfied smile, "Good job, now I'm done!"

Well, you are not finished quite yet! There is one more area in which you can have some positive influence that will encourage the members of the group. This area is celebrations.

It is easy for members of the group to throw themselves into the work they developed and after time look up and feel that not enough progress is being made. This feeling can lead to frustration and unfortunately to a cessation of progress.

It is not easy to find areas to celebrate as you work on the solution to a complicated problem. In fact, one solution may uncover another problem and so on. It is important to build into the group at an early stage the routine of celebrating small successes. This may seem trivial; but far from being extraneous, it is essential to the morale of the group and the success of the overall project. This is especially true with people who have never worked in a group to solve a problem or resolve conflict.

Before we go any further, it is important to emphasize a point. People are quite savvy and will soon see through manufactured moments of celebration. When you are choosing the times to celebrate, the celebrations must be based on easily recognizable achievements that have merit. Otherwise the members of the group will see through the attempt and feel as though they have been manipulated. This will lead to negative feelings, as no one really feels good about being manipulated. So make sure that the moments or achievements you choose to celebrate are seen by everyone as worthy of attention.

This is an appropriate time to provide some examples of moments to celebrate. Please note that these are just examples and that as you work with the group, the moments that warrant celebration will become apparent to you.

Examples of moments to celebrate:

- The group has successfully navigated their first major disagreement by airing all sides of the discussion and finding a consensus solution.

- Some members of the group begin to mention to other members of the group that they are violating the working agreements and ask them to abide by the agreed-upon way of behaving in the group.

- A small group comes back with a "straw dog" for the rest of the group to consider. The group has a fruitful and helpful discussion leading to a solution they can all live with.

- Every member of the group has completed work on his or her own that will help the group move forward when they meet again.

- Members of the group learn to test their assumptions by asking questions such as, *when you say that this is the most important area we must focus on, what you are really saying is . . .*

- Members of the group take on the leadership of the group by successfully serving as facilitators, recorders, as a member of a small group, and so forth.

Hopefully, you get the idea!

The celebration being advocated here is not a large party with balloons, cake, and a clown. Rather, it is recognition by the members of the group for a genuine achievement. Typically, an honest and enthusiastic round of applause is all that is necessary for people to feel honored.

The facilitator can say, "I've been noticing that you are all helping one another abide by the working agreements. Thank you for working together to help make this a safe place." Another example, "Tara, Fred, Eugene, and Margaret did a complete job of developing the straw dog for the group to examine. Would you four please stand up? Let's give them a round of applause."

As you can see this does not have to be a long involved process, but rather an honest expression of appreciation for a job well done. The facilitator's role in this process is to look for authentic moments to celebrate and then model the process. The hope is that the group will catch on and begin offering small celebrations independently. You will know that you have succeeded in instilling this concept in the group when one member of the group asks to speak to the entire group and then shows appreciation for another member.

During the first few times you choose to celebrate the achievements of members of the group, you may want to explain your thinking behind the small ceremony. By simply stating your intention to thank members of the group for their courage or hard work, people become aware of the meaning of the celebration and are less apt to dismiss it. Coupled with the fact that the event being celebrated is based on authentic achievement, it is likely that the members of the group will feel encouraged to participate in future celebrations.

It is quite possible as you begin this process that the member of the group being honored will feel self-conscious and awkward. This is a natural response, especially in groups that do not know each other well or in organizations in which celebration is not a part of the culture. In this instance, by practicing the art of celebration, people become used to it and at some point even expect it.

So keep at it for a while and monitor the reactions of the group. If they are not warming to the activity after five or six attempts, you may consider stopping it. Before you stop it for good, have an honest conversation with the group about what you are doing and why.

Knowing the reason behind an activity will sometimes help ease the way to acceptance of its use.

You may be thinking that reading about celebrations in this way is a waste of your time. It is important to note that working adults are often guilty of overlooking the achievements of others. This is typically not done with ill intent. Rather, we just get too busy doing the work that we do not look up to notice what is going on around us.

While looking for authentic occasions to celebrate may feel forced at first, keep reminding yourself that the work these folks are doing is difficult. Anything you can do to encourage them is well worth the time spent.

This is not to say that there are not times when a big celebration is in order. If the group has found doable consensus solutions to a complex problem, it may very well be the time for a cake and maybe some ice cream. Of course, just like the rest of the decisions about the work that the group is doing, it is up to the members of the group to organize the celebration. Be careful that you do not take this concept into your own hands. If you have modeled celebrations and the group declines to participate on their own, accept that fact and move ahead with the agenda.

Just like planning ahead to include working agreements, purposes, decision-making procedures, and appropriate interventions, planning for celebrations at the beginning of the process is useful because you are prepared to use it from the start. However, it is really never too late to include authentic celebrations in the work you are doing with the group.

The important point to remember is that the item or work that inspired the celebration must be seen as a real achievement rather than a staged activity. Your job as a facilitator is to explain the purpose for the activity, model the process, and encourage members of the group to use it, as well.

Concepts to Consider

- Celebration of authentic achievement is important to encouraging the hard work of members of the group.

- The celebration process is a simple recognition of a job well done that publicly mentions the people involved and their achievements followed by a round of applause.

- At the beginning of the process, the facilitator may choose to explain the reasons behind the use of celebrations.

- While the facilitator starts and models the celebration process, it is his or her hope that the members of the group will take up the process and celebrate their achievements.

NOW THAT YOU'VE FINISHED THE PROCESS, IT IS TIME TO START OVER
(Included is a description of the process for data conversations about student achievement)

It may be discouraging to you to read the title of this chapter especially after you have successfully shepherded a group of people to a successful outcome. The truth is that the event that you just designed and facilitated was just the beginning of a much longer process. Rarely does one event or intervention completely solve the problem or conflict. This is especially true of complex problems or long-running conflicts you will most likely be asked to facilitate.

The trick is to explain to the decision-making authority at the beginning of the process that you are prepared to facilitate the group to a successful conclusion of the immediate problem, but they should be prepared that further work may be needed.

It should be stated up front that this is not intended to be a ploy for more work for you. It is the nature of complex problems or deep conflicts that they have many layers. As you peel off or solve one problem it may lead to another problem and so on.

In addition, if the work that the group has done is to be sustained, it will require constant monitoring and adjustment. Ideally, the members of the group are prepared to work on the problem for the long term and are eager to take on the responsibility of assessing results, examining the data, evaluating the interventions, and making changes if the data supports it.

It is incumbent upon you as the facilitator to work with the group members about the need for developing an awareness of the implementation of a continuous progress model. This model was first developed by W. Edwards Deming for the Japanese at the close of World War II, and it explains a process for continually monitoring the work by looking at data produced by the project and making adjustments or changes as a result of the data (learn more at www.deming.org).

Simply put, the continuous improvement process uses the wisdom of teams to identify and solve a problem. At the heart of the process is the collection and analysis of data about the problem. Using the Current State/Preferred Future process, the team will develop Next Steps to lead them from the Current State to the Preferred Future.

Implementation and the monitoring of the next steps is the first part of the continuous improvement process. The members of the team will gather data about the implementation and then determine its effectiveness.

It is essential for groups and decision makers to understand the continuous improvement process and to realize that the work they are doing will be part of a larger ongoing project. The good news is that once a group has been through the full length of a facilitated event they have a better understanding of the work it takes to resolve complex problems.

In addition, the members of the group have confidence that they can discuss difficult situations successfully. They also have confidence that they can work successfully with people who may hold vastly different views. This experience will provide them with the tools and knowledge to continue the problem-solving process.

The Role of the Facilitator in the Continuous Improvement Model

The first and foremost role the facilitator takes is teacher. Throughout the process of facilitation you've designed, you have been teaching the members of the group several important lessons. Here is a list of lessons taught through the facilitation process.

Participants learned

- To speak honestly and openly in a safe environment.

- The processes that allow each person to be heard.

- How to successfully facilitate small groups.

- How to record the comments of each person.

- Not to make decisions based on assumptions, but rather test assumptions.

- To honor the ideas and wisdom of each member of the group.

- To feel confident that they can solve complex problems with other people.

- To build in evaluation and accountability processes to ensure that the work they commit to is successfully completed.

- How to come to consensus.

- That consensus means that their voice was heard in the discussion, they can live with the decision, and they can support the decision publicly.

This is just a partial list of the concepts that participants learned as a result of your facilitation. All of the items on the list and those not said will enable the members of the group to successfully continue the process in the future.

The second role of the facilitator in the continuous improvement process is the inclusion of the evaluation and accountability sections of the facilitation work. By including these sections and guiding the group to use them, the facilitator is setting up the continuous progress cycle. This is true because the group has agreed to monitor and adjust the solutions and interventions they developed over time.

The third role of the facilitator is as coach. You will find yourself in the many aspects of coaching, including encouraging, teaching, modeling, developing a strategic plan, and celebrating small wins.

As the facilitator of the group you are in a unique position. You are not a part of the group and therefore not responsible for making decisions on their behalf, and yet, the members of the group look to you for direction and advice. Because you are not bound by the constraints and politics of the larger organization, you can provide honest and unbiased feedback to the group about the way they are working with one another and the issues you see as important.

Lastly, as a coach, you have some measure of emotional distance from the group and can provide important insights by holding up a proverbial mirror to the behaviors and issues of the group. In this way the group members can see the implications of their behaviors using that information to adjust the work they are doing.

Using Facilitation Concepts *and* Continuous Improvement Models to Increase Student Achievement, an Example

One of the best applications for the combination of the facilitation process and continuous improvement is in schools. The current trend in education is to have teachers collect relevant student achievement data, examine the data, and make adjustments to their instructional focus to better target instruction so students can learn at high levels.

Teachers are learning the process of ongoing formative assessments and are certainly creative and experienced in using multiple instructional techniques. However, not every teacher or group of teachers is skilled at facilitating a process that allows them to successfully talk about the data, draw conclusions, and collectively adjust teaching strategies to better target students needs.

There are many experts who have developed extensive plans and technologies that allow teachers to create, grade, and analyze student achievement data. The focus of these programs is on the data. Data is only one part of the process.

Teachers need to work collaboratively with one another to analyze that data, sometimes noticing and responding to troubling trends, and then design strategies based on the results of the data analysis to adjust their instruction. A problem can occur when a group of teachers sit together to discuss the data and disagree about the meaning of the data, the methodologies used to collect the data, or which strategies to implement. If they do not have the skills to successfully facilitate a difficult discussion, the entire process will stop.

The good news is that just as teachers can learn to expertly analyze data, they can learn to facilitate difficult conversations with their colleagues. The skills and practices outlined in this book are the foundation of successful collaborative process designed to help teachers discuss difficult issues. Clearly these skills are not complex and are as useful in a data conversation as they are in a large problem-solving conversation.

Outlined below are the steps that teachers can take to design a process in which difficult decisions are discussed and effective interventions are developed. These conversations can be achieved in an environment of mutual respect and understanding.

Setting up the environment for effective conversations about student achievement data:

1. Make sure that the purpose of the group and purpose of each meeting is clearly understood.

2. Identify how the purpose of the group connects with the larger purpose of the school.

3. Develop or adopt working agreements.

4. Decide on a decision-making model.

5. Choose to have the above items on the agenda every time you meet.

6. Use a shortened version of the Current State/Preferred Future process to examine data.

    a. The Current State is the place where the group examines the student achievement data, taking turns identifying their interpretation of what the data means.

    b. In the Preferred Future section, the teachers will define at what achievement level they want the students to perform and what success will look like.

    c. During the Next Steps section the teachers brainstorm and agree on strategies that lead them from the Current State to the Preferred Future.

7. The teachers agree to implement the strategies developed during the Next Steps section of the process.

8. After the identified period of time allotted for the interventions to work, the teachers collect the data and meet as a group to analyze how closely the students came to meeting the identified achievement targets.

9. If the students have not made the progress teachers had hoped, different strategies are brainstormed and implemented, and the data are examined collectively.

10. If the achievement targets are met, the teachers identify the next area of concern and start the process all over again.

The first six steps of this process are key to ensuring a safe environment in which to have, at times, difficult discussions. The development of the safe environment is often overlooked. In that case, the data analysis process may work just fine for a while, but at some point the discussion will turn serious. It is at this point that the establishment of purpose, working agreements, and a decision-making process will help the teachers navigate the rocky waters of disagreement.

As teachers work with one another using this process, their confidence will grow and they will be more likely to take on the big issues that are affecting the achievement of their students.

As they begin to see that by monitoring the data and adjusting instruction, all students are improving their achievement, they will be inspired to continue the process. While many of us do not like to attend meetings, those meetings that bring about a doable plan are much more pleasant to attend.

Concepts to Consider

- Many times the initial facilitation event is the beginning of a longer process especially when confronting complex problems or deep-seated conflict issues.

- The use of a continuous improvement process will help a group to examine progress on initiatives and make adjustments during the implementation process.

- Facilitators serve three important roles in the continuous improvement process as teacher, effective role model, and coach.

- A shortened Current State/Preferred Future process is quite useful for educators who are implementing data talks to improve student achievement.

CHAPTER TWELVE

WHAT DO YOU DO IF . . . ?
STRATEGIES TO DEAL
WITH GROUP ISSUES

The purpose of this chapter is to provide the reader with reasonable and effective strategies to employ when a member of the group is acting in a way that is contrary to the good of the group. It is important to note that the first step to solving the problems that may occur with disruptive group members is to head them off—with the development of working agreements, a clear understanding of the purpose of the group and each meeting, the careful selection of group members, and a clear, doable decision-making strategy as these elements provide the foundation for a safe environment in which the group will work.

However, even with the best planning and foresight, members of the group may act contrary to the working agreements and exhibit disruptive behaviors. Let's face it, you will be working with people who may be unpredictable.

Disruptive situations and possible solutions are written below. In addition, tips for facilitators are included as a guide for you while you work. There is no guarantee that these strategies will solve every problem. However, they have been used successfully with several diverse groups.

Dealing with Disruptive Behavior

Problem: Interrupting others.

Solution: The most basic solution to this problem is to structure the conversation so that each person shares his or her ideas one at a time.

However, some people may interrupt during discussions or brainstorming sessions.

Strategies:

1. Try is to stop the person who is interrupting by simply stating, "Excuse me, Jim, it is important to let Leslie finish her thought. I'll come back to you in a minute." Most times one reminder will be enough to resolve the problem.

2. If Jim's behavior persists, your next step is to talk with him privately about his behavior, reminding him of the need to ensure that everyone feels safe in the group and asking him to wait his turn.

3. Once in a great while, the person who interrupts is expressing frustration that he or she is not getting a chance to speak. You may discover that the structure you've designed is not allowing everyone a chance to speak. In this case, adjust the process you are using to ensure each person's chance to speak.

4. One last proactive strategy to consider is calling on people during a discussion so that they know they will get a turn to talk. It might sound like this, "Gosh, there are many hands up. Let's start with Marie, then Rasheed, and on to Rebecca." That way the participants know they will have a turn, which relieves their anxiety about getting their point out in the open.

Problem: Side conversations.

Solution: If you review the working agreements mentioned earlier in this book, you will not find "no side conversations" listed. The no side conversations concept is embedded in the working agreement of Treat Each Other with Respect.

A simple reminder from the facilitator, "We decided at the beginning of the process that we would treat one another with respect. That means that it is important to listen to each comment silently with respect," typically solves the problem.

Strategies:

1. Talk to the offending group members during a break, letting them know that you have noticed that they are having side conversations, which is not respectful to the entire group, and ask them to stop.

2. People having side conversations may be sending a message to you as facilitator that they need time to process what is being said. In this case, you will want to build in time for people to discuss what was just presented. This can be done simply by instructing the group members to speak to a partner to answer these questions, *Does what was presented make sense to you? What questions do you have?*

Problem: A person chooses not to participate.

Solution: The first thing to determine is whether you have structured the process so that there is an opportunity for every person to participate. If this is the case, and the person still refuses to participate, it is important to remember that you can't make people do what you ask them. Each person has the choice to participate or not. It is important to speak to the person during the break to determine the reason he or she is choosing not to participate.

If the reason has to do with the structure that you could change without disruption, then consider doing so. However, sometimes people are angry about another issue or don't want to be a member of the group. In this case, remind them that you welcome their participation and hope that they will choose to become involved.

In rare cases, the person who is not participating may choose to leave the group. If he or she chooses to leave, remind yourself that people make their own decisions. You can leave the door open for them to return should they want to, but do not go after them or beg them to stay.

Each person has a right not to participate. Sometimes having the person in the group who does not participate is a distraction. The group may be more productive without them as a member. Please don't misunderstand; this is not a call to get rid of disruptive members of the group. Rather, it is an acknowledgement that some people may choose not to participate, which is their right.

Problem: A group member argues with the facilitator.

Solution: Remember that it takes two people to engage in an argument. As the facilitator, you must guard against engaging in an argument with members of the group.

Strategies:

1. Remember that you were asked to facilitate the group. The hiring authority decided that you and the process you outlined would help move the group to a successful solution. Typically, a member of the group who argues with you about the process is less interested in the process and more interesting in asserting his or her authority or control.

2. You can deflect this challenge relatively easily by saying to the challenger, "There are many ways we could proceed from this point. However, I've outlined a process that I am confident will help us get to our goal. I intend to continue with the outlined process." By saying this you are establishing that you are in charge of the group. Most times this reminder is all that is necessary to solve the problem. Once in a while, a group member will persist.

3. Speak to the person during a break about his or her behavior. Once you've had that conversation, stay strong; proceed with the process you've outlined and ignore the challenging comments.

Problem: Members of the group do not follow your instructions.

Solution: This may occur in small groups with members of the group who are not familiar with the process you have outlined. Typically, members of the group need a little coaching from you to conduct the process correctly.

Strategies:

1. If you are working with a large group, which you've distributed into smaller groups, you will monitor them as they work. If you see a group that is struggling with the process, stand near them and intervene only long enough to redirect them. You may say something like, "Let me remind you of the instructions. Start with one person letting him or her share and then on to the next person and so on until everyone has a chance to report their ideas." The point is to get them on the right track and then let them take over the group. Usually, just a few minutes to redirect the group does the trick.

2. If you see that several groups are struggling with directions, don't hesitate to stop everyone and review the instructions. One thing that people new to facilitation do is to present too many directions at one time. It is better if you can break your directions into smaller chunks, especially at first. It doesn't do any good to let a group struggle for an extended time. Intervene after a short period of observation and then let them get back to work.

Problem: Negative body language.

Solution: During the early 1990s there was much written about the meaning of body language and how to read it. I find that it is quite difficult to accurately read another person's body language. Rather, if one of the group members is sitting with arms and legs crossed and a frown upon his or her face, look for secondary signs of a problem.

Ask yourself these questions: Are they participating in the activity? Are they a productive member of the group? Do they follow the instructions you've given? Do they follow the working agreements? If the answer to these questions is yes, then don't worry about crossed arms and legs. If the answer to the questions is mostly no, then follow the suggestions in the section above for when a person chooses not to participate.

Strategy:

1. It is too easy to misread the body language of other people. If the person is not disruptive, then ignore the body language. If they are disruptive, deal with the issue directly. Don't spend a great deal of time analyzing body language. You've more productive things to do. Crossed arms may mean someone is cold!

Problem: The meeting is interrupted by cell phone calls.

Solution: It is appropriate to expect that when people attend a facilitated event that they will participate fully. Having a cell phone ring and a group member answer it is disruptive. It also sends the message that there are more important things to attend to than the current meeting.

If you are involved with group members who are used to having access to their cell phones at all times, it may be difficult for them to turn the phone off. However, it is both respectful to the rest of the group and the process to request that cell phones be turned off.

You may need to make a specific announcement to the entire group. If it is one person who is using the phone during the meeting, ask to meet on a break and inquire why it is necessary for him or her to use the phone during the meeting. If at all possible, politely request that the phone be turned off. If there is a legitimate reason for the cell phone to be on, you may ask him or her to share with the entire group about needing the phone on and, if appropriate, provide a reason.

It is better to inquire privately about the reason for the phone use rather that trying to guess at the reason. I was a participant in one group at which we were asked to turn off our cell phones for the duration of the meeting. During the opening activity, a woman shared that while she understood the reason we were asked to turn off our cell phones, she was keeping her phone on because her mother was quite ill and wasn't expected to live much longer. We all understood at once and accepted her request.

Problem: Group members arrive late or leave early or both.

Solution: The first step is to make sure that group members understand the importance of fully participating in the group. Remind them that full participation means that they arrive on time and are ready to work. Sometimes a general reminder will solve the problem.

If the problem persists with one or more individuals, take them aside during a break telling them that you've noticed they are having difficulty arriving on time and that when they are late it is disruptive. During the conversation, you will most likely learn the reasons for the tardiness. After hearing the reasons, you can encourage the person to try to be on time or you may need to counsel him or her out of the group.

There are times when people want to participate, but are overextended. They may need to make a choice about whether participation in the group will work for them. Remind them that if they should choose to continue with the group, they will need to avoid disrupting the group by arriving on time and staying for the entire meeting.

Problem: Members of the group are doing many things during the meeting: grading papers, knitting, sending texts, drawing.

Solution: When members of the group are attending to something other than or in addition to the work you ask them to complete, they may be sending the message to the rest of the group that the work you are doing is not as important as their work. There are many people who are great at successfully completing two or three tasks at once. However, the concern is less about the person doing two or three things at once than with the rest of group members who are participating fully. Those group members are giving their full attention to the task and expect their colleagues to provide the same courtesy.

This is an issue that can be resolved by a quick reminder of the working agreements, especially, Participate Fully. If members persist in this behavior, speak with them during a break about the distracting behavior and ask them to stop grading papers, knitting, drawing, or whatever.

Problem: A group member makes comments quietly after others speak.

Solution: This behavior is a violation of the working agreement Treat Each Other with Respect.

Strategies:

1. Make sure that the process you are using allows everyone to have his or her voice heard.

2. You can remind the entire group about the issue of respect.

3. Speak to the offender at a break reminding him or her that the comments he or she is making are being overheard and are not respectful.

You may get the feeling after reading this section that facilitation is full of problems. The reality is that it is not! However, by setting up the conditions for a safe environment, many of the problems will not ever occur. If they do, you can always refer to the working agreements to remind people that you all agreed to abide by them at the beginning of the process.

Of course, it always helps to be prepared should something like the behaviors listed above arise. Your best move is to address the issue quickly while not embarrassing anyone or disrupting the group. Remember, you can always call for a break to address an issue in private should you need to make the time.

Tips for the Facilitator

In this section you will find a list of tips that are intended to be helpful to you as you start your work with groups. Some of the tips will resonate with you immediately while others may be useful later.

Tip 1: Don't Take the Disruptive Behavior Personally

It is often the case that a disruptive person is acting out his or her own issues through disruptive behavior. Of course, there is no way to see inside a person's brain or to truly understand the reasons for the behavior. However, when you personalize the disruptive behavior by thinking *he or she is doing this on purpose to frustrate me*, you have activated the part of your brain responsible for emotions. From this state of mind, it is hard to make reasoned decisions about next steps. For the most part, as a facilitator, you need to move above the fray and address the disruptive behavior coolly and rationally in order to avoid escalation of the situation.

Tip 2: Do Not Be Afraid to Confront People Behaving Badly

It is often a learning point for new teachers when they are told or realize that their job is not to befriend each student in their classes, but rather their job is to teach the students. The same dynamic can happen among facilitators. You may feel that you are working on a difficult situation that requires tact and patience and as a result you ignore disruptive behavior such as interruptions or side conversations to engender the good will of the group members.

It is just as important for you as facilitator to realize that you are not there to befriend the members of the group as it is for the new teacher to realize he or she is not there to befriend the students. You are hired to design an environment that is emotionally and physically safe for everyone in the group.

To do this effectively, you must confront disruptive behavior as it occurs lest it gather momentum. Sadly, the consequence of not confronting disruptive members of the group effectively is the loss of a safe environment and eventually loss of respect for you as the facilitator. While this situation can be resolved, it is more difficult to do the longer it persists.

Tip 3: Take a Break If You Need It

Sometimes facilitators are caught up in the agenda and timing and may feel as though they must push through even if an incident occurs. Remember that you are the one who decides the timing and duration of any breaks the group takes. There is nothing wrong with giving the group a five-minute break while you deal with an issue or adjust the process. Simply tell the group that they may take a break and then deal with the issue. Yes, even if they had a break just a few minutes ago. It is better to deal with an issue immediately rather than letting it fester or escalate.

Tip 4: Scan the Group as They Are Working with Your Eyes, Ears, and Intuition

As the group is working, you will have the opportunity to observe them as they work. You can pick up clues to how the group members are feeling by watching them, listening to the comments, and following your gut.

For example, you will know when the group is working seriously on a task based on the sound level. A group deep in conversation sounds like a small rumble. As the group is finishing their work, you will hear louder voices and laughter signaling to you they are ready to move on.

Of course, seeing a number of the members of the group with puzzled looks on their faces may be a clue to you that they are unclear about the task or instructions. Simply ask for their attention and say, "I've noticed that several of you are looking puzzled. Can I assume that you are confused by the directions?" The group will let you know if they need clarification.

If you feel as though something is not quite right, trust your intuition. After getting the attention of the group, tell them of your unease and ask them to let you know if they are feeling it as well. Most likely, the group members will either reassure you that all is well, or they will confirm your feelings. It is far better to ask than to move ahead not knowing.

Listen carefully to the comments that group members make during the opening and closing activities. They will reveal many things about how the group members are feeling, what issues are on their minds, whether they think the group is making progress, and so on. Use this knowledge to adjust your plans. It is easy to say to the group, "Gosh, it seems like many of you are wondering where we are headed. I am glad to know that so I can clarify the path for you."

The more often you facilitate a group, the stronger your intuition becomes regarding issues in the group. However, as highly refined as your intuition is, you need to confirm your feelings by asking members of the group about your concerns. By being open and honest with the group, you are learning what you need to know and modeling for them how they can express themselves or challenge assumptions.

Tip 5: Try Your Best to Ensure That the Work the Group Is Doing Will Get Implemented

There is nothing more demoralizing than working hard with a group over difficult issues, developing a reasonable set of recommendations or next steps, and then having nothing happen to solve the problem. The group feels as though they were pawns in a game rather than authentically dealing with an issue. Unfortunately, morale can sink to even lower levels than before the intervention began.

While there are no guarantees in facilitation, it does help tremendously if before you even begin you get an agreement from the hiring authority that the work of the group will be used productively. This conversation may seem premature. However, you want to make sure before you even begin the planning for the facilitation that your work will lead to a change in the identified situation. If the hiring authority is vague on this point or delays a response, you may want to think twice before proceeding with the facilitation. It is a waste of everyone's time if there is no concrete plan to implement the work of the group.

While you will have little control over the final project, it is better to know that those who are in authority take the work that you are about to undertake seriously. Of course, there are times when the best plans and interventions have to be put on hold because of unforeseen circumstances. Group members may ask you, "Is this work really going to make a difference?" You want to honestly answer, "Yes."

Tip 6: Facilitate in Packs

As was stated at the beginning of the book, it is very possible for one person to successfully facilitate groups up to eighty people. However, two or three heads are better than one. The larger the group, the better it is to have a colleague or two sharing the facilitation task with you. The other facilitators will notice things that you may miss and suggest strategies that you had not thought of. So if you are in the position to share leadership of the group and you trust the people you are working with, then the more the merrier.

Tip 7: Get Help If You Need It

It is clear that you will want to facilitate the group your way and you should. However, even the most experienced facilitators will come across problems or issues they are not sure how to handle. Don't be shy about asking for help. It is much better to reach out for a different perspective than to suffer through a difficult problem. Make the call to someone you trust and ask for help or to check your assumptions!

Tip 8: Don't Make Decisions about the Process Based on Assumptions

If you are sensing a problem or feel uncomfortable, check your assumptions with the group. You are so much better off when you have checked your assumptions and use that information to help guide your work. Even the very best facilitators get their wires crossed once in a while. Rather than act on your assumptions, clarify them! The group will be glad to help!

Tip 9: Trust the Process

Most of the people you will be working with have not had experience with a skilled facilitator. You were hired because of your skill and expertise. Your plan will work if you have done your homework and truly understand the context and the problem. It sometimes takes time for the process to work fully. Group members may become confused about the activities that you ask them to do. If they express that confusion, explain the process and the reason for it.

Tip 10: Be Flexible!

Having just said to trust the plan, it is equally important to adjust the plan when new information or unexpected situations are encountered. You would be foolish to continue down a path that will not lead you to a successful solution. If you must change strategies, do so based on firm data rather than assumptions. To reiterate, you are paid to be the expert in the process. If you find the need to divert from your original plan, then by all means do it!

You may be thinking at this point, "Yikes, what did I get myself into!" This feeling is totally understandable. Remember that this book is intended to be a resource as you facilitate. As many issues and tips as could be imagined were included in the book so that it would be a strong reference for you. Some of the things listed above you may never encounter. Other things will become clearer as you gather facilitation experience. The bottom line is to believe in and trust your instincts and knowledge!

Concepts to Consider

- The best solution for disruptive behaviors is to preempt them by establishing clear working agreements, purposes, and meeting structures.

- The working agreements are in place to ensure that the facilitation meetings will be held in a safe and supportive environment. You will return to and emphasize them as you address disruptive behavior.

- Try to make sure that you deal with disruptive behavior quickly, respectfully, and with cool detachment.

- Remember that you are the one in charge of the process. You can modify the path you are on based on new information and data.

- The tips for the facilitator provided in this chapter are a resource to you as you complete your work.

- Test your assumptions before acting on them.

CHAPTER THIRTEEN

RESOURCES FOR FACILITATORS

The purpose of this book is to provide the framework for a successful facilitation event. The previous chapters have described the important foundational elements needed by the facilitator to structure the process. The Current State/Preferred Future template was described in detail.

The purpose of this chapter is to explain some of the resources available for use by facilitators as they plan their work with groups. There are several books filled with protocols and processes promising to solve all kinds of presenting problems. Without the foundation of elements described in this book, there is no guarantee that the use of the protocols and processes will lead to success. However, any protocol has the chance to lead a group to a successful conclusion when the elements of effective facilitation are used.

As with most jobs that have at their core working with people, it is best to have a number of procedures that are useful for different groups. Most likely, you will find procedures that you feel comfortable with and use regularly. However, make sure that when you first talk with the hiring authority, gathering information about the presenting problem or issue, that you are open to reviewing several protocols to find the one with the best chance of leading to a successful outcome.

Of course it is impossible to mention all of the resources that will inform your facilitation practice. However, the resources listed here are time tested and proven to work. Some of the resources listed are for general reference or to add to your knowledge of facilitation. Others are describing protocols and procedures that you can use with groups. All are chosen because they are written by experts in the field with many years of successful experience facilitating groups.

No doubt you will find other sources of information that are useful to you as you do this work.

The resources below are divided into two general areas: reference and procedural. Reference materials are added because they will provide structural knowledge and skills about facilitation. Procedural materials will provide templates and protocols you can employ right out of the book or modify to fit the needs of your group.

Reference

Flawless Consulting

Peter Block wrote the quintessential book about consulting entitled *Flawless Consulting: A Guide to Getting Your Expertise Used*. It was first published in 1981. The wisdom found in these pages is timeless. Peter Block provides great advice to the consultant within the organization and when you are a consultant from outside the organization. This book is valuable because it provides complete instructions about how to negotiate a contract and how to consult so that the work done makes a difference; it also includes descriptions of how consultants for all areas can work successfully. The most valuable part of the book is Peter Block's emphasis on being a consultant of character and conscience. Doing things the right way is on every page.

Details:

Block, P. *Flawless Consulting: A Guide to Getting Your Expertise Used* (1981), Pfeiffer and Company, San Diego, CA.

Peter contributed to an updated version of his classic book entitled *The Flawless Consulting Fieldbook and Companion: A Guide to Understanding Your Expertise*. This volume was published in 2001 and contains advice and information from Peter Block and thirty flawless consultants. This book is also filled with the wisdom and experience of the people who are successfully consulting each day.

Details:

Block, P. *The Flawless Consulting Fieldbook and Companion: A Guide to Understanding Your Expertise* (2001), Jossey-Bass/Pfeiffer, San Francisco, CA.

The Skilled Facilitator

Another great resource for the art of facilitation is *The Skilled Facilitator* written by Robert Schwarz. In this complete reference you will find many explanations of the work of facilitation along with descriptions of the process and the reasons why it is important. This is a great reference book to have handy when you are first beginning your facilitation work and to browse when you have encountered an unfamiliar problem. There is an updated version entitled *The Skilled Facilitator Fieldbook*.

Details:

Schwarz, R. M. *The Skilled Facilitator* (2002), Jossey-Bass, San Francisco, CA.

The Fifth Discipline and Schools That Learn

The next two selections are both reference and procedural because in the pages of these books you will find an explanation of processes and activities that you could use with groups. Both of the books come from the groundbreaking work of Peter Senge in his classic, *The Fifth Discipline*. Dr. Senge was one of the first people to publish a book explaining a model of systems thinking.

In the books *The Fifth Discipline Fieldbook* and *Schools That Learn*, Peter Senge and his collaborators describe how his innovative ideas outlined in *The Fifth Discipline* are interpreted and implemented. *Schools That Learn* was written for the express purpose of assisting educators and those who care about education to work toward positive improvements. Using these books as a reference is quite helpful and may stimulate and challenge your thinking.

Details:

Senge, P. M., Kleiner, A., Roberts, C., Ross, R. B., Smith, B. J. *The Fifth Discipline Fieldbook* (1994), Doubleday, New York.

Senge, P. M., Cambron-McCabe, N., Lucas, T., Smith, B. J., Dutton, J., Kleiner, A. *Schools That Learn* (2000), Doubleday, New York.

Procedural Resources

Facilitating with Ease

Ingrid Bens describes several processes for facilitation in her book *Facilitating with Ease*. The protocols described in the book will help you guide groups through many aspects of facilitation, including, but not limited to, data gathering, problem solving, conflict resolution, and decision making.

Details:

Bens, I. *Facilitating with Ease* (2000), Jossey-Bass, San Francisco, CA.

The Adaptive School: A Sourcebook for Developing Collaborative Groups

Robert Garmston and Bruce Wellman are expert facilitators who have helped thousands of groups meet their goals. They wrote a book published in 1999 entitled *The Adaptive School: A Sourcebook for Developing Collaborative Groups*. This book offers great advice about how to facilitate groups so that they achieve their goal of transformational change. Included in the book are many different facilitation strategies you can use to help groups move forward.

Details:

Garmston, R., Wellman, B. *The Adaptive School: A Sourcebook for Developing Collaborative Groups* (1999), Christopher-Gordon Publishers, Norwood, MA.

Bob Chadwick's Procedures

Helping groups to resolve long-standing and deep-seated conflicts is one of the most challenging facilitation jobs. However, Bob Chadwick has been helping diverse groups to resolve their conflicts successfully for thirty years. Bob's first career was as a forest superintendent for the U.S. Forest Service in the northwest. During his tenure he was constantly dealing with major conflicts between logging companies and environmentalists, Native American tribes and dam operators, mining companies and logging companies, and many other groups.

Bob developed a process for conflict resolution out of his experience working with these groups. His process gets people from opposite sides of an issue in the same room to work out their differences. It works. People from diverse backgrounds with suspicion of one another are able to hear each other, find common ground, and develop strategies to move toward long-term solutions.

Bob has not written his procedures in a book you can purchase. The only way you can learn the procedures he developed is to attend a workshop designed to lead participants through the process, thus learning it themselves. Consensus Institutes are held at regular intervals. If you find yourself in a situation where you are asked to help people with deep-seated conflict work toward a resolution, you will want to learn these techniques.

Details:
Bob Chadwick
Consensus Associates
P.O. Box 235
Terrebonne, OR 97760

As with any subject, there is much to learn about facilitation. Hopefully, the resources listed above, along with this book, will give you a good place to start successfully facilitating groups. Know that people who make facilitation look easy are very good at what they do. You may find yourself working with a group for the first time worried that something will go wrong. Trust yourself, follow the processes outlined in this book and others, be authentic, and get to work. You can do it!

Concepts to Consider

- While there are many valuable resources one can access to learn about facilitation process and protocols, the bases of any facilitation events are the concepts contained in this book.

- There are books that are designed to provide protocols for you to use. There are other books as well that are terrific for providing background information.

- Excellent facilitators make the work they do look easy. However, there is a structure and purpose to their work.

- As a facilitator it is important to continually seek out new ideas to add to your facilitator's toolbox.

MATERIALS FOR SUCCESSFUL FACILITATION

W hile the facilitator does not need as many tools as a carpenter or plumber, there are many materials that ensure that the facilitation event will proceed smoothly. This short chapter will describe the different materials a facilitator will likely use. While brand names are not included in the description of the product, after a quick search and a bit of experience, the most usable items can be located.

Chart Paper

The use of chart paper is traced back to Kurt Lewin and his colleagues who were conducting a serious negotiation in the 1940s and wanted a way to record what was being said for all to see. One night when planning for the next day's session, as the story goes, he had the bright idea of getting some white butcher paper from a local shop to write down the work for the next day. The rest, as is often said, is history.

In some cases, chart paper has been used for every meeting in an organization and the employees tire of seeing it on the walls. Others might say that in the digital age it is a waste of resources. It is hard to find a better way for each small group to quickly record their responses for everyone to see. Of course, these responses will be transcribed at a later time.

There are many types of chart paper produced. Some have lines and others are plain. It doesn't much matter what brand you use. The only consideration is that it detaches from the pad easily. Trying to detach the used pages off the tablet without tearing them is not always easy.

Chart Paper Markers

Look for markers that say they are made for chart paper. Many permanent markers will bleed through the top page and mark the next page making it unusable and wasting paper. Another consideration to consider while purchasing markers is smell, as many people are sensitive to strong smells. Always choose markers that have little or no odor.

Discard empty markers when you discover them in the pack. Having several colors in the package you give to groups to use is fun. However, take out the yellow markers. While useful for many things, they do not show up well on a chart people are trying to read from across the room.

Several manufacturers produce marking pens for use with chart papers. After you buy some and use them, you will discover which brands work well.

Even if the organization you are working for has agreed to supply markers, it is best to carry some of your own. You may not know which markers will be provided and they may not work. It is better to carry a few packages of your own just in case they are needed.

Chart Paper Stands

Easily the most cumbersome and awkward tool you will use during facilitation is the chart paper stand. These stands come in many shapes, sizes, and weights and are designed to hold the chart paper pad upright so it is easy to write on. Typically, the chart paper stands have either a clamp to hold the pad or pegs to slip through the holes on the top of the chart pad.

The sturdier the chart stand is, the better. You certainly don't want the stand to fall over under the weight of a full pad of paper or for it to tip over while someone is writing on it. So the chart stands with relatively thick legs and a solid back are the sturdiest.

Some manufacturers market a portable chart stand. While these are easy to carry, they are basically three telescoping aluminum tubes that come together at the top where a clamp is located to hold the pad. These are typically not very sturdy and for the most part should be avoided.

The best situation is to have the hiring organization provide chart stands and pads for the facilitation. You will need one for every small group. If you are working with a group of twelve or less, one chart stand is sufficient. This is an item, unlike the markers, that is difficult to move from place to place.

It is better to have the chart stands at the event site rather than bringing them yourself. Many convention sites, meeting rooms, and hotels will rent them for a nominal fee or provide them free of charge with room rental.

Tape

You may choose to display the pages the participants have written on the wall for all to see during the meeting. The easiest way to attach the charts to the wall is by using tape. Most folks reach for simple masking tape to accomplish this task. Resist this idea! Masking tape, while good at holding up the chart, may take paint off the wall. It is better to use painter's tape, typically blue, or artist's tape, typically white, because they are designed to hold an item securely and then release cleanly. Artist's and painter's tapes are more expensive than masking tape, but they will save you problems in the long run. Lastly, it is a good idea to carry a roll of artist's or painter's tape with you to the facilitation. It is relatively small and portable.

There is a useful activity called "the gallery walk" during which participants of the session walk around the room reading all of the charts much like viewing paintings in an art gallery. Once participants have viewed the charts you can have them develop a set of themes that are common in all of them.

Another great use of the activity is to have the entire group review the information before making a decision or prioritizing next steps. Of course, this cannot be accomplished without the use of tape to hold the charts to the wall.

3 by 5 Cards

You will find that a staple of the work you do in facilitation is the 3 by 5 note card. On this card you will have participants write their responses to many of the questions you will ask. The note cards have the advantage of being small and sturdy. They are easy to write on, even if the only writing surface available is your leg or lap. There is no advantage to lined or unlined cards and color is not important. Plain, white 3 by 5 cards are the simplest and easiest to use.

It is a good idea to add a stack of these to the briefcase or bag that you bring to the facilitation. While the hiring authority can provide them for you to use, it is better to have some just in case in the preparation for the day they are forgotten. They are portable, small, and easy to carry.

A Computer

You will find that having access to a computer with a word processing program or bringing your own is useful for typing up the responses on the charts for the group to review at the next session. This kind of transcription is especially useful for groups when they are looking for themes or prioritizing comments or if you want them to have read the documents before the next meeting. If you are lucky, someone from the organization for which you are working will be assigned to transcribe the chart!

One quick note about transcribing the comments from the chart paper is that it is important that you transcribe the comments exactly as they are written on the chart. This is to preserve the exact thoughts of the participants as they were said to the recorder. The only corrections you will make is to make sure the words are spelled correctly.

During the transcription is not the time to worry about correct grammar. That will come at a later time when a document is being prepared for public consumption. Lastly, type the comments in random order. The group will do the work of prioritizing and/or finding themes. Let the group know that the comments were typed the way they were written with the exception of corrected spelling.

You may find that having basic office supplies with you (rubber bands, paper clips, extra pens and pencils) will be useful. Filling your facilitation bag or briefcase with a small number of these items will ensure that you have the things you need and eliminate the process of searching for them during the session.

As mentioned at the beginning of the chapter, the materials used are far from the most important part of the facilitation experience. However, just like any job, using the correct tools makes the work go much easier.

Concepts to Consider

- Having good tools makes the session run smoother.

- Assembling a "facilitation bag" with these items will ensure that you have them when you need them. You can quickly grab the bag when you head out for the session.

- Asking the hiring organization to provide chart paper and charts stands, enough for the group size, is a helpful idea. These items are bulky to carry and store.

- Some of the tools you may need are
    - Chart paper
    - Chart paper markers
    - Chart stands
    - 3 by 5 file cards
    - A computer
    - A small quantity of office supplies such as paper clips, rubber bands, extra pencils and pens.

ABOUT THE AUTHOR

Steven A. Schiola is a thirty-year veteran of Colorado public schools. He taught at the elementary level for nineteen years. He served as the staff development coordinator for Poudre School District in Fort Collins, Colorado, for seven years. For the last five years of his career he served as the principal of Cache La Poudre Elementary in Laporte, Colorado.

Steve has successfully facilitated well over seventy events for public and private schools, school districts, businesses, government agencies, university departments, and community and nonprofit organizations. He is founder of Open Road Consulting, LLC, based in Fort Collins, Colorado.

In addition to facilitating events, Steve enjoys reading mystery novels, playing with his puppy Leonardo, traveling, skiing, playing the banjo, and hosting a bluegrass show on a local community radio station. He lives in Fort Collins, Colorado, with his family.

For more information, visit the author's website at www.open roadllc.com.

Breinigsville, PA USA
30 September 2010
246375BV00003B/1/P